HRM Sample Materials

Cases, Problems & Designs on Human Resource Management (HRM) Topics

Clare A. Francis
University of North Dakota

ISBN 10: 1515176835

ISBN 13: 978-1515176831

Preface

This book has been designed as a resource for instructors, trainers, learners, supervisors and managers. It may accompany traditional Human Resource Management (HRM) textbooks to provide hands on tools to support learning experiences. The ultimate aim is to stimulate learners' creativity to design original sample materials to improve HR practices in organizations.

Each chapter begins with two brief discussions. One introduces the HR topic with cause and effect relationships. The second differentiates high quality versus low quality HR practices on the HR topic. All chapters contain sample materials related to one or a few specific HR practices to demonstrate how a small part of HR functions in a firm. Seven of eleven chapters have cases to consider HR issues in organizations. Chapters also include activities such as problems to solve and HR designs to create for high quality HRM practices. The first five chapters present broad topics in HRM: the HR field, HR strategy, legal issues, organizing work and employee turnover. For example, Chapter 4 on Organizing the Work suggests numerous HR practices to improve how work is arranged to motivate individuals and groups. Chapters six through eleven present core HR topics including recruiting applicants, hiring candidates, training employees, conducting employee appraisals, designing employee pay and incentive plans. For example, Chapter 6 considers the process to recruit job applicants. Learners are given guidance on information necessary to create a high quality job ad. They are asked to prepare a job ad for a specific job title. A second topic is on sources of job applicants: specific outlets such as university career centers, print media, and online job boards. Learners are asked to create a list of recruiting sources with contact information for the job title in the ad they created. Finally, recruiting metrics are discussed with a presentation of numerous specific metrics and sample calculations to show a hypothetical firm's experience in recruiting. The metrics provide important guidelines for future recruiting campaigns. They also give insight on the quality of sources of job applicants to identify those more likely to provide candidates who will be high performers for the firm.

Most HR concepts are based on management research. Cases, HR problems to solve and designs to create are based on the author's experiences over several decades in consulting, management, and in training employees and students. Materials were developed to give insight to readers on how to prepare sample documents for HR programs in general. The goal is to help improve HR functions in work settings.

Acknowledgments

Many former students and former and current colleagues have contributed to the ideas in this book. As a teacher, I am also a learner and wish to thank students for valuable insights I continue to gain in the classroom. I wish to also extend special thanks to colleagues for their encouragement and support, Sean Valentine, Kathy Jones and David Hollingworth in the Department of Management at the University of North Dakota.

Disclaimer

This book is for educational purposes. Any employee information represents fictional characters, and does not refer to actual persons. Statements are not interpretations of laws or regulations and should not be construed in any way as legal advice or legal services. Laws continually change and are interpreted by judicial branches of governments and others. It is suggested that organizations engage legal experts as needed on HR topics.

CONTENTS

Overview of Main Chapter Sections VII

CHAPTER 1 HUMAN RESOURCE MANAGEMENT (HRM) FIELD 1

Case: Should a Small Company Hire an HR Intern? 2
Sample Materials: HR Design on Division of HR Duties 3
1st HR Problem to Solve: Division of HR Duties 4
2nd HR Problem to Solve: High or Low Quality HR Practices... 5

CHAPTER 2 HRM STRATEGY 7

Case: FTEs & Scheduling Plan... 7
Sample Materials: HR Design of FTE Analysis for Different Staffing Configurations 8
HR Problem to Solve: Staffing Insight with FTE Analysis 8
HR Design to Create: Prepare Sample Materials for an FTE Analysis 9

CHAPTER 3 LEGAL ISSUES IN HRM 11

Case: 80% Rule – Test for Evidence of Discrimination in Hiring 12
Sample Materials: HR Design on Analysis of the 80% Anti-Discrimination Rule 12
1st Problem to Solve: Analyze Hiring Results for the 80% Rule – Your Company 13
2nd Problem to Solve: Hiring Results for Two Managers.. 14
HR Design to Create: Prepare Sample Analysis for Evidence of Discrimination 15

CHAPTER 4 ORGANIZING THE WORK 17

Case: High Supervisory Turnover 18
Sample Materials: HR Design on Self-Managed Work Teams 19
1st HR Design to Create: Prepare an Original Sample Detailed Job Description................20
2nd HR Design to Create: Prepare an Original Job Design using the Job Characteristics Model...........................21

CHAPTER 5 EMPLOYEE RETENTION 23

Case: Poorly Trained Supervisors and High Employee Turnover 23
Sample Materials: 1st HR Design on Cost of Turnover 24
HR Design to Create: Prepare Sample Skills Inventory Database to Facilitate Retention ... 26

CHAPTER 6 RECRUIT JOB APPLICANTS 27

Case – Part A: Recruiting Mistake in Search for Technology Specialists 28
Case – Part B: Recruiting Decision Based on Metrics to Hire from the Best Sources 28
Sample Materials: HR Design of Recruiting Metrics by Source of Applicants 30
HR Problem to Solve: Calculate Metrics for Two Sources & Identify Best Source of Three 30
1st HR Design to Create: Prepare a Sample Chart of Employee Performance by Recruiting Source 31
2nd HR Design to Create: Prepare an Original Sample High Quality Job Ad......................... 32
3rd HR Design to Create: Prepare List of Sample Sources & Contact Info to Recruit Applicants 33

CHAPTER 7 SELECT & HIRE JOB CANDIDATES 35

Case: Negligent Hiring & Screening Applicants to Identify Candidates for More Testing ... 36
Sample Materials: Screening New Hires in Settings with Vulnerable Persons 37
Framework for Structured Behavioral Job Interview Questions with STAR Method............ 38
Sample Materials: Structured Behavioral Interview Questions & STAR Rubric – Past Behaviors........39

1ST HR Design to Create: Prepare Original Sample Structured Interview Questions for a Job Title 40
Sample Materials: HR Design on Work Sample Test Protocol 42
2ND HR Design to Create: Prepare a Work Sample Test Protocol 44
Sample Materials: HR Design to Validate Tests -Track Scores for Hiring Tests & Performance 45
HR Problem to Solve: Rank Job Candidates with Multiple Test Scores 46

CHAPTER 8 TRAINING EMPLOYEES **49**

Sample Materials: HR Design on Orientation Training for New Employees 50
Sample Materials: HR Design on Self-Management Training-Sales & Customer Service Reps 52
Sample Materials: HR Design on Verbal Self Guidance (VSG) Training 54
HR Design to Create: Prepare a Sample Plan for On-the-Job Training (OJT) 56

CHAPTER 9 APPRAISE EMPLOYEE JOB PERFORMANCE **57**

Sample Materials: HR Design of Job Duties Mapped to Work Standards & Goals 58
Sample Materials: HR Design of Work Standards 59
Sample Materials: HR Design of Individual Employee Performance Appraisal 60
HR Design to Create: Prepare Sample Performance Appraisal Materials 61

CHAPTER 10 COMPENSATE EMPLOYEES **63**

Sample Materials: HR Design of Generic Pay Structure with Grades & Ranges 64
Case: Red Circled Roland 65
1ST HR Problem to Solve: Collect Market Wage Data for Retail Job Titles 66
2ND HR Problem to Solve: Update Market Wages to Estimate Future Wages 67
HR Design to Create: Prepare a Unique Sample Pay Structure for a Small Retail Outlet 69

CHAPTER 11 EMPLOYEE INCENTIVES **71**

Sample Materials: HR Design on Simple Individual Bonus Pay 72
Problem to Solve: Simple Individual Bonus Calculation 72
Sample Materials: HR Design on Individual Pay with Scorecard 73
Problem to Solve: Individual Bonus with Scorecard 73
Sample Materials: Work Group Incentive – Gainsharing Program 74
Problem to Solve: Work Group Incentive – Gainsharing Program 75

REFERENCES **77**

- ○ Introduction with Discussion of Cause and Effect Relationships

Since the 1930's researchers have been identifying cause and effect relationships involving employees in the workplace (Mayo, 1947) as part of the early "Human Relations Movement." These efforts addressed various topics including interactions between employee, peers, and supervisors. The early experiments showed that humane treatment, two way communications between workers and leaders, and group involvement led to higher employee productivity. This movement was the forerunner of today's Human Resource Management (HRM) field. HR research is ongoing around the world and seeks to identify employee programs that contribute to firm success.

- ○ Discussion of High versus Low Quality HR Practices

In all organizations with employees, HR activities are occurring whether HR staff are present or not. For example, in small businesses owners recruit and hire job applicants, train employees, compensate employees and more. How are those processes being done? The response might be, "we do what everyone does." This suggests average quality HR processes at best. Average operations do not result in competitive advantage. More successful organizations pay attention to research and data to help drive decision making. The HR field has grown to provide managers and business owners the ability to improve HR practices. Each chapter of this book presents a few research tested HR practices as examples to enhance HR programs.

- ○ Sample HR Materials

The sample materials are shown to stimulate learners' creative abilities. The goal is to present a few materials to encourage students' to develop original sample materials for other problems they encounter. Sample materials may support recommendations to upgrade HR practices in organizations.

- ○ HR Problems to Solve and HR Designs to Create

Problems and designs contained in the book give learners hands on experiences to work with HR concepts. Ultimately, the purpose is to give learners tools and experiences to be effective in organizations and to contribute new ideas to help improve HR processes.

[Intentionally Blank]

Chapter 1 Human Resource Management (HRM) Field

Introduction with Cause and Effect Relationships

Most firms divide HR duties among numerous persons, some with HR training and others without. Each organization tends to have a unique set of HR methods given the variety of experiences among different supervisors and managers. Research shows the quality of HR practices impacts organizational success. Higher quality HR practices tend to support more favorable outcomes than lower quality HR practices.

A rigorous research study by Huselid (1995) was based on survey responses from senior HR professionals in over 800 publicly held firms of 100 or more employees and represented most major U.S. industries. Survey questions in Huselid's study addressed the extent firms engaged in the following HR activities:
- recruited high numbers of applicants per vacancy & tested job candidates to hire
- trained employees
- appraised employee job performance
- based pay and bonuses on merit & promoted from within
- formed employee work teams & shared company information with employees
- conducted employee attitude surveys & gave employees access to grievance processes.

Huselid correlated the level of firms' HR activities with employee turnover, sales per employee, the firm's market value per employee and profits per employee for each firm. In general, the results showed more favorable outcomes for organizations with a greater extent of high quality HR practices compared to firms with lower quality HR practices.

High versus Low Quality HR Practices

Huselid (1995) determined the impact on organizations by comparing results for firms with low versus high quality HR practices and systems. Statistically significant results showed that a small incremental increase in high quality HR systems could improve organizations with lower quality practices each year as follows:
- Decrease annual turnover by 7%
- Increase in sales worth $27,044 per employee
- Increase in market value worth $18,641 per employee
- Increase in firm profits worth $3,814 per employee

The effects of high quality HR practices shown above represent results for one year. In general the effects of HR practices accumulate over time with results extending over the long term. Improved firm outcomes are not guaranteed by implementing higher quality HR practices. Outcomes depend on the design of HR programs and systems and how well they are implemented. Each chapter in this book considers the quality of HR practices.

Case: Should a Small Company Hire an HR Intern?

Pat Sullivan, owner and president of Custom Industrial Products, Inc., (a hypothetical firm) was pleased with the company's continued growth and success in recent years. The company was small with 65 employees. They designed, manufactured and sold industrial products to major U.S. firms. The company had generous profit sharing and bonus plans for employees. Overall annual pay for each employee was well above market rates. The company had low turnover and easily attracted new talent. However, at times employees complained about the lack of clarity on vacation time, holidays, and a variety of other employee matters. Pat was concerned about the lack of an employee handbook. He and his managers, along with clerical and accounting staff shared all HR duties.

Pat felt he and the company were not ready to hire full time HR staff. He had a long standing personal policy that each new hire should at least "pay for himself or herself." He felt a full time HR staffer would not generate revenue for the company. His Controller suggested he check with the local university about internship programs. Pat discovered the college of business had a major in Human Resource Management. Faculty indicted that senior level HR students would be interested in applying if he offered an internship program.

Pat was not convinced an HR intern would be a good investment and decided to meet with his top managers. The Directors of Marketing, Engineering and Design, Operations and Accounting were each responsible for part of the HR duties. Pat himself annually reviewed market wage rates to set raises for employees. It was a tedious task and he sometimes felt unsure that his decisions were logical. Pat and his top managers had difficulty at times keeping up with the HR tasks since the client base was growing and product orders were increasing every quarter.

Pat asked the managers what they thought about hiring an HR intern. What duties could they expect to assign to an HR intern? The managers were quiet at first, until the Marketing Director blurted with excitement that he would have more time to work with clients and could generate more sales if he could delegate HR duties to an intern. The Engineering and Operations Directors agreed. They also could be more efficient. It occurred to Pat that an effective HR intern could INDIRECTLY increase revenue and improve operational efficiencies by giving his talented managers time to focus on product designs, sales and operation of work units.

1. Should Pat hire an intern for a semester, assuming qualified applicants are available? Explain why or why not.

2. What type of HRM duties could be delegated to an intern?

3. Assume the intern gives them "a small incremental increase in high quality HR practices." Although, favorable firm results are not guaranteed, consider Huselid's (1995) research. Use a conservative estimate of one-tenth of his dollar findings for increased sales per operational employee per year for 40 of Pat's 65 employees. The firm is in a growth cycle. Hypothetically, how much could sales increase by hiring an HR intern and assuming HR programs are designed and implemented well?

4. Assume the intern works 1,000 total hours for $12 an hour for one year (about half time) and the company includes him or her in employee benefit programs at a cost of about 20% of wages. Do you think it could be a good investment to hire an HR intern?

Sample Materials: HR Design on Division of HR Duties

Table 1.1 HR Duties Shared by Managers in Different Sizes of Organizations

HRM Duties	Less than 100 Employees: HR Duties assigned by Job Title	100 to 500 Employees: HRM Duties assigned by Job Title	More than 500 Employees: HR Duties assigned by Job Title	You are a Manager, what size firm? Mark items below with "My Tasks"
Recruiting Systems	CS	HR	HR	
Place & Write Job Ads	CS-MM	HR-JM-MM	HR-JM-MM	
Hiring Systems	CS	HR-CS	HR	
Job Interviews	MM-SM	HR-JM-MM	HR-JM	
Job Specific Training	JM-MM	HR-JM	HR-JM	
Appraisal Ratings & Meetings	MM-SM	JM-MM	JM	
Pay Systems	MM-SM	HR-MM-SM	HR-MM	
Pay & Promotion Decisions	MM-SM	MM-SM	JM-MM	
Benefits	MM	HR-JM	HR-JM	
Safety	MM	SS	SS	

Legend: HR: HR Staff; CS: Clerical Staff-Non HR; JM: Junior Managers / Supervisors; MM: Middle Managers; SM: Senior Managers - Owners; SS: Safety Specialist.

Explanation of Table Entries
- Companies with less than 100 employees do not usually employee HR staff.
- As expert HR systems are developed, Junior Managers can be trained to share more HR duties
- System HR tasks are duties behind the scenes. For example recruiting includes identifying sources to find applicants, maintaining contact with them. Hiring systems include screening candidates, testing, arranging interviews, etc.
- Operational HR tasks include candidate interviews, employee training and more.

QUESTIONS TO ANSWER:
1. What size firm do you expect will be your employer after graduation?

2. Indicate in the far right column of Table 1.1 the HR duties you expect to have in your first job as a manager. If you currently are a supervisor or manager, what HR responsibilities do you currently have?

1st HR Problem to Solve: Division of HR Duties

Talk to a Manager and ask who is responsible by job title to do various HR tasks. Talk to persons with job titles such as owner, president, manager, supervisor, HR manager-staff, accounting managers and more.

For all questions focus on <u>one non-supervisory job title</u> for the organization, such as a cashier, sales associate, server, cook, bank teller, personal banker, landscaper, pet groomer, hair stylist, baker, carpenter, mechanic, etc.

For example, for question 1 below ask a manager: "Who by job title is responsible to recruit job applicants for cashier positions?

    A. Indicate the company's industry:

    B. Indicate the approximate number of total employees in the company:

    C. Indicate the approximate number of employees at the location of your inquiry:

    1. Who recruits job applicants, places job ads?

    2. Who screens, tests, interviews job candidates?

    3. Who conducts general employee training such as orientation training?

    4. Who conducts employee training for job skills?

    5. Who appraises employee job performance?

    6. Who makes pay and promotion decisions for employees?

    7. Who explains benefits to employees?

    8. Who conducts disciplinary meetings with employees?

    9. What do you conclude overall, who shares responsibility for HRM tasks in general for this firm?

2nd HR Problem to Solve: High or Low Quality HR Practices

We recommend organizations implement high quality HR practices to improve employee productivity, turnover and financial results. HR practices include methods to recruit and hire employees, to design jobs, to create quality teams, to share company information with employees and to train employees, to conduct job performance appraisals, to pay and promote employees based on merit, and to provide employees with access to formal grievance procedures.

Think of a company you know well and identify specific high or low quality HR practices that you believe may have had a favorable or unfavorable impact on organizational outcomes. HR practices are listed in Table 1.1 above and also in the 1st Design to solve. Examples of outcomes to discuss may include one or more of the following:
- Employee productivity
- Employee skills and abilities
- Employee attitudes
- Employee attendance and turnover
- Customer service
- Product quantity and / or quality
- Gross sales and /or profits
- Expenses and / or waste
- others

1. What is the company's industry?

2. What is the approximate market area, local, regional, national or global?

3. What HR practice do you believe impacted an outcome? Explain if you feel it was done in a high or low quality manner?

4. What company outcome do you believe was impacted?

[Intentionally blank]

Chapter 2 HRM Strategy

Introduction with Cause and Effect Relationships

One part of HR strategy and planning is to analyze inputs and outputs per a standardized unit of the workforce. A Full Time Equivalent (FTE) employee is a metric frequently used in many industries. One FTE is defined as the hours worked by a standard full time employee, 40 hours per week for 52 weeks per year, equal to 2,080 hours per FTE per year. A small business with 10 part-time employees each working 20 hours per week for 52 weeks per year computes FTEs as follows: 10 persons x 20 hours per week x 52 weeks = 10,400 total employee hours per year. The workforce size stated as FTEs would be calculated by dividing total employee hours divided by 2,080 hours: 10,400 hours / 2080 hours = 5 FTEs. Imagine a company with 80 employees. Most are full time, a few are half times and very few are less than half time. The company calculated employee hours for the year were 149,750 hours. Total FTEs for would be 149,750 / 2,080 = 71.99, about 72 FTEs. FTEs are used to compare work units on different results such as revenues, expenses or productivity.

High versus Low Quality HR Practices

The FTE metric is a standard basis to compare various outcomes. For example, a manufacturing company with plants in different regions of the country may compare average expenses per FTE and average units produced per FTE to assess plant efficiency and productivity. The FTE metric gives firms the ability to identify business units that operate more successfully. HR practices in the more effective business units may then serve as models to consider implementing in business units with less favorable results.

Firm inputs and outputs are often compared within an industry. A company as a members of an industry associations may elect to submit confidential data to the association. Associations use the information to produce industry reports on average results across firms. Data in the industry reports mask company names and identifying information. This allows the association to distribute reports to member firms. Managers in each firm may determine their relative position in the industry on various data points. Common ratios to compare within an industry include average sales per FTE, average payroll expenses per FTE, units produced per FTE and more. They also can compute percentiles for companies to indicate outcomes for firms in the top versus bottom tiers for each data item. FTE analysis serves as a critical input to make business decisions.

Case: FTEs & Scheduling Plan

Barb & Brothers Mfg. Inc. (a hypothetical firm) produces a small catalogue of standard mechanical parts for the auto industry. Three plants in three different states produced nearly identical products. The firm gave full time employees a generous package of benefits, bonuses and profit sharing. Part-time employees received a similar package on a pro-rated basis for hours worked. Different amounts and types of training were offered in the different plants. Plant managers also had different job performance appraisal methods and different staffing configurations. All plants have the same quality requirements with few product rejections. Plant #1 hired only full time production employees, 40 hours per week, 52 weeks each year. Plant #2 hired only part-time production employees, 20 hours per week, 52 weeks each year consisting of persons wanting shorter work week such as persons nearing retirement, college & technical school students, parents with children and others. Plant #3 had two staffing configurations: full time employees with a reduced schedule of 35 hours per week, 52 weeks per year. In summer the plant hired a 2nd shift of college students to work 30 hours per week for extra summer orders. See Tables 2.1 and 2.2 for FTE calculations and analysis of output results and units produced per FTE.

Sample Materials: HR Design of FTE Analysis for Different Staffing Configurations

Table 2.1 FTEs and Staffing Configurations in Three Manufacturing Plants

Plant #	# employees	Hours per week per employee	Weeks Worked Per Year	Total Hours Per Year All Employees	Total FTEs for Year
1	100	40	52	100 x 40 x 52 = 208,000	208,000/2080 = 100
2	150	20	52	150 x 20 x 52 = 156,000	156,000 / 2080 = 75
3a	87	35	52	87 x 35 x 52 = 158,340	158,340 / 2080 = 76.1
3b	60	30	14 Summer	60 x 30 x 14 = 25,200	25,200 / 2080 = 12.1
3 Total	147	35 & 30	52 & 14	158,340 + 25,200 = 183,540 (Sum 3a + 3b)	183,540 / 2080 = 88.2

Table 2.2 FTEs and Production Output in Three Manufacturing Plants

Plant #	Total FTEs per Year (Table 2.1)	Units of Output per Year	Calculate Output per FTE per Year	Output per FTE per Year	Rank by Output per FTE, 1 = Best
1	100	65,000	65,000 / 100 =	650	
2	75	47,000	47,000 / 75 =	626.6	
3a	76.1	54,850			
3b	12.1	9,990			
3 Total	88.2	64,840	64,840 / 88.2 =	735.1	

HR Problem to Solve: Staffing Insight with FTE Analysis

QUESTIONS to ANSWER based on data in Table 2.2

1. Indicate in the far right column in Table 2.2, plant rank based on the plant's average output per FTE.

2. Explain possible reasons for differences in the productivity, assume the strict quality requirements were maintained in all factories. Why might the most productive plant have better results than plants with lower productivity?

3. Plant 3 has interesting results. Are the full time workers more productive or the summer college students? Complete the analysis of Output per FTE per Year for 3a and 3b in Table 2.2. Enter your results in the second column from the right for rows 3a and 3b in the blank cells. What might the owners do to better understand the results? What might be follow up steps to take in other plants?

Assume you are working for an organization with five retail outlets in five similar geographic markets. They each have different work schedules and types of employees (full time, part-time, students, retirees, veterans, with and without job experience) The different outlets provided different incentives to employees and different amounts of professional training for supervisors. Managers in the various outlets share company information differently with employees and provide different types and frequency of feedback to employees on work performance.

Two outlets struggle with sales volume, overall profits and customer satisfaction scores. Other outlets continue to improve with increasing sales, profits and customer satisfaction. Display a chart with hypothetical data to show the owner of the five outlets how he or she could clarify the different results by using FTE analysis. For example, a company can calculate gross revenue per FTE, total expenses by FTE, payroll expenses by FTE, profits by FTE, training hours per FTE, bonuses dollars earned per FTE, etc. Assume successful outlets use higher quality HR practices compared to the lower performing outlets. Assume all outlets are located in pleasant suburban areas with robust economic conditions and growing populations.

PREPARE A CHART OF ANALYSIS Similar to Table 2.2 based on hypothetical data to compare results of five outlets. Label headings and show calculations to demonstrate how FTE analysis can provide insight to owners & managers.

[Intentionally Blank]

Chapter 3 Legal Issues in HRM

Introduction with Cause and Effect Relationships

In 1964 major federal legislation was passed in the U.S. Laws made discrimination based on race, religion, gender and national origins illegal for employment decisions. Additional laws have been passed to expand and clarify earlier legislation. The laws require employers to assess job candidates on job related criteria and ability to do essential job tasks instead of on gender, race, religion or national origin. The laws apply to many employment decisions. For example, employers are required to be fair in offering employee training, in giving job performance appraisals, in making pay and benefits decisions. The laws do not permit employers to exclude persons from fair processes because they belong to an ethnic or religious minority, are women, older persons, or military veterans. Each employee has rights to file complaints against his or her employer with the Equal Employment Opportunity Commission and to sue an employer for unfair treatment based on race, religion, national origin and gender.

Research shows that firms with anti-discrimination programs to build an inclusive work place tend have more favorable outcomes compared to firms with discriminatory practices. For example, in a study involving over 4500 health sector employees Downey, van der Werff & Thomas (2015) found employees had more trust in managers and higher commitment to the company in firms with higher levels of diversity programs. A large U.S. retailer participated in a research study conducted by McKay, Avery, & Morris (2009). They analyzed 654 retail outlets of the company and found higher overall retail sales in outlets where employees viewed the company had higher commitment to diversity compared to outlets where employees viewed low commitment to diversity.

High versus Low Quality HR Practices

Research studies provide statistically significant evidence to indicate that diversity programs and initiatives to build an inclusive workplace are higher quality HR practices and tend to support favorable business outcomes. Discrimination on the other hand may contribute to lack of trust among employees and managers, and lower employee engagement. These less favorable results may be associated with other employee outcomes. Discrimination can result in complaints and law suits by employees against employers. Lawsuits tend to draw press attention and can harm a company's reputation and firm success.

Equal Employment Opportunity Commission (EEOC) STATISTICS:
Despite the laws, discrimination continues to occur across the U.S. in work settings. Below is a summary of statistics on discrimination charges filed with the EEOC by individual employees and groups of employees. Detailed statistics by year for over 15 years are available at eeoc.gov. Annual statistics on monetary benefits granted to victims paid by employers resulting from lawsuits and settlements and are also available at the website. A few data items are shown below.

Number of Charges Filed for Discrimination at Work:

	2000	2013	Increase	% Increase
Race	28,945	33,068	4,123	14.2%
Gender	25,194	27,687	2,493	9.9%
Religion	1,939	3,721	1,782	91.9%
Disability	15,864	25,957	10,093	63.6%
Total Charges, all categories	79,896	93,727	13,831	17.3%

Employers paid over $1.1 billion to victims in discrimination settlements from 2000 to 2013
  (eeoc.gov /eeoc/statistics/enforcement/charges-a.cfm)

Case: 80% Rule – Test for Evidence of Discrimination in Hiring

The owners of Rex & Muffin Food Processing, Inc., a hypothetical firm, launched several new pet food product lines in recent years with rapid growth in demand. The company's two plants are in different states near farms that supply product ingredients. Each plant is also within 40 miles of a metropolitan area with ample workers to staff the plants. Each plant has added a 2nd shift and a new production line to meet increasing demand. Last year managers frequently submitted orders to HR staff to fill vacancies for new production positions. HR staff were busy recruiting and screening applicants for managers to consider hiring.

Pat Wilson the HR Director at headquarters monitors HR staff in the plants. She reminded them to recruit in a variety of labor markets to attract diverse applicants in terms of ethnicity, gender, age, etc. The owners are strong supporters of diversity and fairness for job applicants and employees. Before the expansion, Pat conducted training for supervisors on Anti-Discrimination laws and EEOC guidelines for hiring. She had stressed the need to hire based on job skills and job experience. She instructed them on the EEOC's 80% rule. Basically, a company is deemed to be within the laws when the selection rate to hire qualified minorities is at least 80% of the hiring rate for the majority group. However, it seemed some minority groups that were represented in the communities and in the pools of qualified applicants recruited by HR staff were not being hired by a few managers as frequently as Pat expected. See Table 3.1 for Pat's overall analysis of hiring results by two racial minority groups.

Sample Materials: HR Design on Analysis of the 80% Anti-Discrimination Rule

Table 3.1 Analysis of 80% Rule to Test for Evidence of Discrimination in Hiring, Rex & Muffin Firm Results

	Actual Hiring Of Caucasians	Actual Hiring of African Americans	Actual Hiring of Hispanics
1 Total # Qualified Applicants	200	50	60
2 Total # Hired	140	30	18
3 Selection Rate (to hire)	140 / 200 = 70%	30/50 = 60%	18/60 = 30%
4 80% Test: Minimum Rate to Hire Minorities	70% x 80% = 56%	Not Applicable	Not Applicable
5 Evidence of Discrimination: Yes/No?	Not Applicable	No Evidence	Yes, strong evidence
6 Explanation: Hire at least 56% of minority applicants to meet the 80% rule & avoid claims of discrimination		60% is higher than 56%, the 80% rule for this firm	30% is lower than 56%, the 80% rule for this firm

QUESTIONS to ANSWER

1 Are Pat's concerns about potential complaints of discrimination legitimate? Federal law requires firms to submit hiring data similar to information in Table 3.1 to the EEOC each year to review potential discrimination.

2   Explain what the EEOC might require of the company to correct problems if qualified Hispanic applicants who were not hired, file a formal complaint.

3 The discrimination settlement process or a court case in favor of a job applicant, often requires a firm to begin an Affirmative Action Plan (AAP) to increase diversity. In cases with required AAP, the firm also must be audited annually by the EEOC for 3 to 5 years. What might the company experience since they advertise they are a fair employer?

1st Problem to Solve: Analyze Hiring Results for the 80% Rule – Your Company

Table 3.2 Analyze Hiring Results for the 80% Rule on Anti-Discrimination in Hiring

	Actual Hiring Results for Caucasians	Actual Hiring Results For African Americans	Actual Hiring Results For Hispanics
1 Total # of Qualified Applicants	120	45	60
2 Total # Hired	88	28	18
3 Selection Rate (to hire)	A:_____	C_____	E_____
4 80% Test: Minimum Selection Rate for Minorities	B:_____	Not Applicable	Not Applicable
5 Evidence of Discrimination: Yes or No?	Not Applicable	D_____	F_____
6 Explain your answers			

QUESTIONS to ANSWER:

Assume you are the owner of this company with just under 500 employees. Assume your operations are just outside a metropolitan area where the population has relatively high numbers of several ethnic minority groups including Hispanics. The data in Table 3.2 show that HR staff are recruiting qualified minority applicants.

1 Explain any evidence of discrimination in hiring that the data reveals?

2 What are action steps you might take with managers responsible for hiring decisions in the company?

a. Training

b. Policy that requires managers hire qualified minorities; a manager duty in job performance appraisals.

c. Disciplinary measures for poor decision making in hiring

3. What programs can the company institute to encourage and celebrate diversity in the company?

2nd Problem to Solve: Hiring Results for Two Managers

We return to the hypothetical firm of Rex & Muffin Food Processing. Pat Wilson, HR Director, felt the need to drill down to investigate the discrimination further. She conducted a confidential analysis on demographics of new hires by two managers to compare results. From Table 3.1 we know managers had a high number of qualified African American and Hispanic applicants. Managers had training on discrimination and company owners are known to encourage diversity. Yet managers make the final hiring decisions for their work units.

Table 3.3 Confidential Demographic Data Collected by HR Staff on New Hires by Two Managers
See two columns on the far right with "X" indicating the manager who hired each new employee.

Employee	Interview Date	Hired: Y-Yes N-No	Gender	Race*	Age	Religion**	Manager X	Manager Y
1	1/5	Y	M	W	25	P	X	
2	1/5	Y	M	W	28	P	X	
3	1/8	Y	M	W	32	C	X	
4	1/8	Y	F	W	34	P	X	
5	1/9	Y	M	W	26	C	X	
6	1/12	Y	M	W	30	P	X	
7	1/15	Y	F	W	33	P	X	
8	1/20	Y	M	A	27	P	X	
9	1/15	Y	M	W	22	J		X
10	1/20	Y	M	AA	35	P		X
11	1/20	Y	M	AA	33	P		X
12	1/24	Y	M	NA	34	C		X
13	1/26	Y	F	W	25	M		X
14	1/26	Y	M	W	48	C		X
15	2/6	Y	F	A	26	P		X
16	2/6	Y	M	A	37	P		X
17	2/10	Y	F	W	28	O		X
18	2/17	Y	M	W	46	M		X
19	2/18	Y	F	H	23	C		X
20	2/18	Y	F	W	34	P		X
21	2/20	Y	M	H	36	P		X

*Race: AA-African American; A-Asian; H-Hispanic; NA-Native American; W-White; O-other
**Religion: P-Protestant; C-Catholic; J=Jewish; M-Muslim; NR-No Religion; O-Other

1   Explain demographic characteristics of new hires by each manager, X and Y. Do you see any patterns?

2   Explain how well each manager upholds company policies on non-discrimination in hiring.

3   What next steps might Pat Wilson consider doing?

HR Design to Create: Prepare Sample Analysis for Evidence of Discrimination

Data in Table 3.3 highlighted interesting patterns to guide the HR Director in taking remedial actions. At times senior managers avoid problems created by rogue junior or middle managers who treat some groups of employees unfairly. You might see senior managers turn a blind eye and say "We can't prove anything."

In fact, data often exists in an organization to verify different practices by different managers. Data simply needs to be collected and organized in a meaningful way. Hypothetical data can show senior managers how to collect and organize data to identify unfair decisions making. Assume you are aware that a few managers consistently give unfair scores on job performance appraisals and on bonus decisions by favoring a select few based on race and gender. Also, a few managers tend to approve desirable training in valuable skills based on race or gender. A display of hypothetical data can be an important step to point senior managers in a direction to avoid lawsuits, fines, penalties and loss of reputation.

Briefly describe a fictional situation with discrimination in appraisal scores, or discrimination in bonuses, etc. Keep in mind the protected groups include racial minorities, religions minorities, women, persons over 40 years old, military veterans, etc. Create an analysis using hypothetical data for two managers to identify the problem. Use the chart below. Enter column headings for data on employee demographics of the protected groups and data for two managers' decisions, one with fair decision making and one with unfair decision making to show how data could be organized for analysis.

DESCRIBE the FICTIONAL SITUAITON:

ENTER COLUMN HEADINGS and DATA IN TABLE

Employee #						Manager A	Manager B
1							
2							
3							
4							
5							
6							
7							
8							
9							
10							
11							
12							
13							
14							
15							
16							
17							

DISCUSSION: Explain patterns you intentionally created to show problems of a possible discriminatory nature.

[Intentionally blank]

Chapter 4 Organizing the Work

Introduction with Cause & Effect Relationships

In the early 1900's the onset of the "Human Relations Movement" (Mayo, 1947) began to impact business owners. Researchers discovered workers could be more productive if given a participative role, if shown respect and more. These ideas led to discoveries on how to arrange work tasks to be more motivating for employees. For example, early factories were operated for efficiency. Workers were often given one or a few tasks to learn well and do repetitively to avoid mistakes. An employee could be assigned a few similar tasks to tighten screws all day on a factory line and not understand what the completed product was or if tight screws mattered.

Hackman & Oldham's (1980) research found five characteristics of work design that improved motivation when work for employees involved:
- using a variety of skills
- working with whole identifiable parts of products
- understanding the impact tasks had on other people
- having the ability to use discretion to organize work and schedules
- receiving feedback on the quality of tasks performed

These five approaches were named the "Job Characteristics Model" and other researchers found the favorable results predicted by Hackman & Oldham (1980) were valid (e.g. Fried & Ferris, 1987). The first three features gave employees a sense of task meaningfulness, the fourth gave workers a sense of responsibility, and feedback allowed employees to understand the results of their work. These psychological factors, meaningfulness, sense of responsibility and understanding results, translated into work outcomes including heightened motivation, improved job performance and higher employee job satisfaction.

High versus Low Quality HR Practices

Researchers clarified that repetitive, single task jobs were low quality job designs. Such jobs tended to be boring and result in poor work outcomes. The Job Characteristics Model gave managers the ingredients to organize work into higher quality designs. Examples of HR programs that include design features of the Job Characteristics Model are work teams such as quality circles in factories and self-managed work teams in a variety of settings, job rotation, job sharing, telecommuting, flexible work schedules, compressed work week schedules and more (Mathis & Jackson, 2011). The impact of using high quality job designs can be far reaching. For example, job applicants may pursue firms known to have better job designs versus firms with boring job designs. Many large and successful organizations have embraced the Job Characteristics Model. Evidence can be seen in information at company websites under career tabs. Job applicants access this information and see detailed job information via videos, employee testimonials, blogs and job descriptions that include interesting and motivating job designs.

Case: High Supervisory Turnover

The accounting department at a large healthcare company (fictional) had high turnover in the "Supervisor of Accounting" position. The highly qualified candidates hired into the position were prime targets for internal recruitment by managers in other departments. The internal transfers meant quick promotions and higher pay for the new supervisors. Each new supervisor had transferred into a "Manager" role such as the Gift Shop Manager and Manager in Food Services. Jim, the Accounting Department Manager lost three supervisors in less than three years. The accounting staff and Controller had grown weary of the vacancies. Jim had to recruit, hire, and introduce new supervisors to the accounting systems. Jim often had to cover supervisor duties and the Controller had to cover some of Jim's duties. The problem caused Jim to miss a few project deadlines. Company policies required managers to cooperate with transfers to support employee development. Jim struggled with the dilemma as he faced yet another vacancy in the supervisor role.

Anne worked in the HR Department as a Quality Improvement consultant to managers to improve operations. She suggested Jim consider a self-managed work team composed of the accountants if they had ample experience. The team approach could eliminate the supervisor position by delegating responsibilities to the accountants. She advised it would involve training, a period of transition and extra duties for Jim until the accountants were ready for the new responsibilities. She suggested he talk to HR staff Trainers for help with classes they offered on team processes, leadership and conflict resolution. Anne could help with implementation. She showed Jim research evidence that self-managed teams could be successful when planned and implemented well. Anne developed a sample chart (shown in Table 4.1) for Jim to responsibilities for the team.

The Accounting Dept. had 12 employees. Betty, an accountant, had 15 years working at the firm and was considered the head accountant by many in and outside the department. She was mature, respected and well-liked by her colleagues. She did not have the education required for the supervisor role. John also had extensive accounting experience, was a shy yet thoughtful person with good ideas to solve problems. Patty and Jeff were super extroverts, dedicated employees with creative ideas. Conflicts occurred at times between Jeff and John. Mary was a mediator type, with less experience in the department. Most accountants, bookkeepers and clerks had average or above average ratings on performance appraisals but none had experience working in teams.

Jim thought the team approach could be a solution. The staff was experienced and professional. Yet he is unsure they will welcome the idea. He needs approval from the Controller and the V.P of Finance. The VP is an advocate of programs to help staff develop. HR helped her train staff for new work designs in the IT area.

1   Jim needs to introduce the idea to the accounting staff and to his bosses to see what they think. He must find out if HR Trainers have time to work with his staff. Explain what you think he should do next and in what order?

2   Review the HR Design shown in Table 4.1. Explain what you see as the strengths and weaknesses of the roles and duties?

3   Assume HR Trainers are available to train accounting staff for the team and assume Jim receives approval to move ahead on the plan. Indicate a time line of steps you recommend to assure staff have adequate time to learn and practice before they fully launch the team.

Sample Materials: HR Design on Self-Managed Work Teams

Table 4.1   Proposed Team Roles and Duties

Titles of Team Roles	Duties by Team Roles	Service Time per Team Role	Decision Input to Fill Team Roles
Team Leader	Lead monthly team meetings & prepare agenda	Assigned each year, limited to two renewals	Manager Nominates two candidates
	Hold daily huddles on issues of the day as needed.		
	Set work schedules & assignments with staff input		Pass HR skills training
	Set vacation schedules with staff input		Majority of members elects leader
	Appraise staff job performance		
	Serve as liaison-other departments, attend management meetings		
	Prepare quarterly team report for Manager of Accounting		
Staffing Committee (3)	Recruit new team members with HR help	Assigned semi-annually, limited to two renewals	Team leader seeks volunteers
	Hire new members with Manager approval		Volunteers pass HR skills training
	Train new members, orientation, Job skills & accounting systems with training check lists and HR help		Majority of members elect committee
Operations Committee (2)	Monitor & Order supplies	Assigned semi-annually, limited to two renewals	Team leader seeks volunteers
	Manage office repairs with Facilities Dept. support		Volunteers pass HR skills training
	Manage office computer systems with IT support		Majority of members elect committee
Communications Committee (2)	Prepare & distribute communications within team and within Accounting Department	Assigned semi-annually, limited to two renewals	Team leader seeks volunteers
	Take minutes at team meetings, email copies to all		Volunteers pass HR skills training
			Majority of members elect committee

Source on Self-Directed Teams: Bishop & Scott (2000)

1st HR Design to Create: Prepare an Original Sample Detailed Job Description

Job descriptions serve as the foundation for many HR activities: to prepare job ads for vacant positions, to determine required skills the job candidates need. Job descriptions are also input to develop work standards for employee performance appraisals and more. Many smaller companies lack accurate job descriptions. Managers can play an important role by helping create up-to-date job descriptions for job titles in their work groups.

Prepare a full job description for a job title you know well. Include the following headings and details for sections as follows:

> Title & Overview: Job title, Department, Supervisor Title, Full time or Part-time, Shift work (Yes-No), etc.
> Recap of Key Job Duties
> Essential Job Duties & Tasks
> Knowledge & Skills Required
> Education & Experience Required
> Physical Requirements (lifting, long periods of standing, vision, hearing, eye-hand coordination, etc.)
> Working Conditions (extreme heat, noise, cold, dust, chemicals, tight spaces, on high structures, etc.)
> High quality job design features you could propose to improve employee motivation and job performance

See ONET online developed by U.S. Dept. of Labor. It displays a detailed menu of job duties to consider for inclusion in job descriptions for over 900 hundred job titles: www.onetonline.org

> See search window in upper right corner of website.
> - o Enter job title in search window, see list of job title options, select job title that is best fit; see details for tasks, tools, technology, knowledge, skills, abilities, work activities and more including job zone with details on training, education.
> - o Scroll to near bottom of same page, see median U.S. wages, see the link for "State Wages."
> - o Collect data on wages for state and the U.S. for the job title (see low, medium and high wages).

2nd HR Design to Create: Prepare an Original Job Design using the Job Characteristics Model.

FOR EXAMPLE: A JOB SHARING ARRANGEMENT for two PROFESSIONALS or other motivating work designs
For non-supervisory professionals who prefer part-time work, such as consultants, party planners, etc.

1 Indicate job title with list of key duties from ONET, Occupational Network, www.onetonline.org
2 List training topics on how to share duties on different days of week; to do a hand off of work each week.
3 Prepare sample checklist of updates to share on clients, projects, etc. to hand off each week.
4 Display a day by day schedule for the two hypothetical employees for two weeks

[Intentionally Blank]

Chapter 5 Employee Retention

Introduction with Cause and Effect Relationships

Most organizations seek to retain employees. Low turnover contributes to retention of valuable tacit knowledge, unwritten understandings on how things work in a firm. Tacit knowledge grows for employees over time and contributes to organizational effectiveness. Greater tacit knowledge means less need for written manuals and staff to give directions. Lower turnover requires fewer resources to fill vacancies and conduct new-hire training. In the past, a large fast food company had a strategy of high turnover with a goal to keep employee benefit costs down. Benefits in these cases usually do not go into effect until an employee has worked for six to nine months. However, the fast food company found this strategy was flawed. High turnover resulted in less knowledgeable employees who caused unhappy customers. More recently the company decided to reduce turnover by hiring older workers with part-time schedules. Special programs and benefits built loyalty among the seniors; they tend to remain with the company for longer times.

Some leaders may not interact well with employees and cause employees to consider changing jobs (Aasland, Skogstad, Notelaers, Nielsen, & Einarsen, 2010). For example, negative and aggressive managers may use a command and control style, which can result in lower job performance in employees (Ashforth, 1994). Difficult leader behavior often results in employee turnover. Training managers may be part of a solution to this problem.

High versus Low Quality HR Practices

Organizations with high quality HR practices tend to have lower turnover compared to firms with lower quality HR practices (Huselid, 1995). Recall the research study in Chapter 1. High quality HR practices included recognizing employee job performance through merit pay and fair performance appraisals. The quality of the supervisor-employee relationship is critical to retain high performing employees. Researchers have studied employees' views on "perceived supervisor support" (Eisenberger, Stinglhamber, Vandenberghe, Sucharski, & Rhoades. 2002). Surveys addressed whether a supervisor supports an employee in his or her job, cares about his well-being, his goals and values, helps when needed, considers his opinions, etc. Supervisors without training in managerial skills can fail in these areas. The daily reality of a difficult supervisor can be challenging for an employee.

Case: Poorly Trained Supervisors and High Employee Turnover

A small yet growing (fictional) firm was experiencing increasing customer orders. Initially the company had been highly successful with talented designers for the custom furnishings for high end homes, offices, shops, garages, etc. Each year designers developed new designs that expanded the customer base. The training department at headquarters had excellent tools and methods to train installers in local markets to work with customers. The firm was selling in most major U.S. markets. Unfortunately the small factories were not able to keep up with the growth. Senior production workers without supervisory experience were promoted to supervisory positions. The work force grew as the complex but popular designs required new and more complicated production equipment. Finishing processes involved more chemicals and hazardous applications with resins for wood designs and plating substances for metal designs. Employees were on their own, assigned to individual machines.

After two years of expansion the executives began to see key business metrics decline. Product quality from the factories fell. Customers and installers complained of missing or wrong parts. Installers grew frustrated due to angry customers with delayed installations. Sales were slowing. The CEO asked two manufacturing experts to tour the factories located far from headquarters. The consultants found problems. One factory was losing 85% of the workforce every quarter to turnover. Few applicants applied. One of the consultants was a professor at the university campus nearby. He asked students about the company. Their response was immediate: "the word is out on campus, we do not apply there. Injuries happen and they don't care about employees."

The consultants observed that employees seemed afraid of their equipment. Training tended to be a quick and confusing demonstration to turn the machine on and place materials. Equipment manuals were not available. Employees felt unsafe. The few supervisors who talked to consultants were not familiar with the new equipment. The VP of Operations, a highly qualified man, was focused on building a new factory. He was rarely at the factory. Supervisors were responsible to run operations. One clerical person staffed the office. No other staff or managers were assigned to the factory. Budgets were tight. The CEO was unaware of these problems.

QUESTION to ANSWER
See Tables 5.1, 5.2 and 5.3 for a sample of general turnover costs and possible supervisory training programs.

1 Explain the top three recommendations you would make to the CEO if you were a consultant.

2. Recall ideas from Chapter 4 on the Job Characteristics Model. Explain job designs that might help improve factory operations.

Sample Materials: 1st HR Design on Cost of Turnover

Table 5.1 Estimated Turnover Costs: Sample Employee Earning $15 / Hour

Type of Cost	Details on Cost	Cost	Totals
Employee Departure Costs	Administrative Time-3 hours at $20 / hour	$60	
	Employee Time-1 hour at $15	$15	
	Accrued Vacation, PTO-8 days @ $15	$120	
	Subtotal		$195
Vacancy Costs			
	Overtime & Temps, 160 hours at $22/hr.	$3,520	
	Wages saved by turnover, 160 hours @ $15/hr.	$-2,400	
Recruit & Hire New Employee			
	Administrative Time-17 hours at $20/hr.	$340	
	Cost of Job Ads	$400	
New Hire Training	Subtotal		$740
	Training Materials	$50	
	Trainer Time, 16 hours at $20/hr.	$320	
	Manager Time (OJT), 8 hours at $30/hr.	$240	
	New Hire Time, 24 hours at $15/hr.	$360	
Lost Productivity,	Subtotal		$970
New Hire Learning Curve	4 weeks, average 50% productivity		
	160 hours x $15 x 50%		$1,200
Estimated Cost-year, $15/hr. Employees	Est. cost: One employee turnover		$4,225
	25 employees quit: 25* $4,225 require new hires		$105,625

24

Sample Materials: 2nd HR Design to Train Supervisors on Communications

Table 5.2   Topics to Train Supervisors in Proper Employee Communications

Main Topics to Discuss	Details of Steps	More Details
Basic Communications with Employees	Respect	Maintain Dignity of All
	Listen actively	Respond directly to question
	Make eye contact	Show care, desire to help with job problems
Educate on Production Equipment	Current employees	On current equipment
On the Job Training	New hires	Promptly after start work
	All users, new equipment	Promptly after equipment arrives
	Review manual	Give employees ready access to manual
	Demo steps to operate	
	Practice time per employee	With feedback on performance
	Re-check performance next day or so	certify ability to use equipment
	Be available for questions	Follow up a few days after training
	Check in often for questions	
	Give feedback often on job performance	to all employees fairly, individually
Maintain OJT Log	Dates, Times, Attendees	Material covered
Conduct Frequent Morning Huddles	Check in with employees	Share info on clients, production, etc.
	Compliment on targets met	
	Updates on new	
	Give tips to meet new targets	Relate to customers if possible
	Alert on safety updates or issues	
	Ask for questions & input	
Maintain Log of Huddles	Date, time, topics, attendance	Have an employee record information

Table 5.3   Methods to Train Supervisors in Proper Employee Communications

Delivery	Content	Follow Up
Cases	Employee Communications Problems & Solutions	Group Discussion
Videos	Supervisors Communicating with Employees	Group Discussion
Role Play	In pairs practice communicating	Partners Discuss
	Alternate roles as supervisor versus employee	Group Discussion
	Use topics discussed in training	

25

HR Design to Create: Prepare Sample Skills Inventory Database to Facilitate Retention

Skills Inventory Databases serve as a reference for managers to quickly identify employees with necessary skills for new projects. It helps employees develop experience and gain new talents by working in different teams.

Assume the company in "Poorly Trained Supervisor" case eventually returns to smooth operations and lower turnover after major initiatives help solve problems. A skills inventory could possibly help them further as they continue to expand with more complex designs for their growing catalogue of products.

- Prepare a table with headings on key data elements about employees

- Enter sample data on three hypothetical employees to show easy access to talent in the database.

- Tips: basic employee info is important: work unit, education, experience, appraisal ratings, promotion potential, special skills, training completed, certifications, career interests.
- Format: Use a landscape layout and multiple lines for a single employee if needed.

Chapter 6 Recruit Job Applicants
Introduction with Cause and Effect Relationships

Methods to recruit job candidates influence employee job performance, turnover and financial results. When a job ad contains vague information, potential applicants may not understand the job. Many may apply without knowing if they are qualified. The result can be many unqualified applicants. Some ads are placed where few talented candidates are able to view it. If an employer hires from a group of poorly qualified applicants, job performance will be lower. Employees hired may quit when they realize the job does not fit their abilities. In these situations, business results can be less favorable due to errors in recruiting.

Recruiting job applicants and selecting job candidates are closely related activities yet very separate processes. For example, an unfavorable recruiting process can result in one applicant per vacancy. The firm has no choice among candidates, no opportunity to choose the most qualified. Imagine a major league baseball team had one applicant per team position, no choice to compare skills and select the best candidates. The scouting process by sports teams is an excellent way to identify qualified applicants to "try out" for a job.

The recruiting process is often started by a manager who alerts HR staff of a vacancy. The manager provides information on required job skills; HR staff may then begin recruiting. Metrics are very helpful in recruiting. For example, a firm needs to know the number of applicants needed to attract an adequate number of qualified job candidates. For example, the "selection ratio" is the overall number of hires as a % of total initial contacts (Mathis & Jackson, 2011). If past experience says 50 contacts results in 10 qualified candidates on average, the selection ratio is 10/50 equals 20%. Metrics by recruiting source help define high quality recruiting practices.

High versus Low Quality HR Practices

Similar to sports coaches HR staff should consider sources of applicants. Where can we find applicants likely to be high performers? Will we find them through newspaper ads or other sources? Companies with high quality recruiting practices use historical data and analysis to identify the best sources of applicants. For example, college sports teams may identify high school coaches or geographic regions known for skilled athletes. Warroad, Minnesota, a small town near the Canadian border is famous as a source of talented hockey players (Custance, 2014). This concept applies to many career fields. Certain sources result in higher qualified candidates than other sources. Firms seeking highly skilled accountants tend to recruit at campuses where accounting majors have high pass rates on the CPA exam. HR staff must know where to find the talent to do excellent recruiting.

Case – Part A: Recruiting Mistake in Search for Technology Specialists

Julie recently started a job as an HR Generalist for a medium sized company (fictional) operating numerous sports & entertainment venues. Her experience was in employee benefits in banking. Her first challenge in the new job was to recruit three new technology specialists to operate and maintain video, audio, digital systems used at events. Monitors were also in multiple locations in each venue. Julie didn't know where to start. Current technology staff were long time employees that had grown with the firm over time. She placed job ads in newspapers locally and in nearby major cities. Ads were expensive, yet resulted in few qualified applicants. The resumes were very weak.

Julie was unaware of the decline in newspaper readership in recent years, from 41% to 23% (Pew Research Center, 2012). Newspapers can still be a good source for entry level positions, or mass hiring's, but they often are not the best source for a specialized field. Julie had a friend who connected her to technology staff at the local college. She asked where they found qualified applicants. They referred her to a website that rated online job boards by career field. She found a few highly rated job boards for the technology field. She placed her detailed ads on the job boards at a relatively low cost compared to print media ads. Within several days Julie had over twenty five applications, more than half were well qualified. The manager was pleased to see many strong job applicants.

   QUESTIONS to ANSWER:
1 Review the Sample Recruiting Metrics in Table 6.1 below and solve the problem. Explain insights you learned.

2 What can Julie do as the firm grows and hires new employees? How can she become more informed on recruiting sources?

Case – Part B: Recruiting Decision Based on Metrics to Hire from the Best Sources

One day the Dean at a university with an MBA program rated in the top 25 in the U.S., received a call from the office of the North American VP for HR in a Fortune 100 manufacturing company. The VP wanted a face to face meeting with the Dean but did not give a reason. The Dean was puzzled. The company hired about ten of their MBA grads each spring. The VP arrived and after introductions, he quickly moved to the topic of hiring MBAs.

The VP told the Dean the company had been tracking new hire data for over ten years. The database gave the company detailed information on job performance and promotion results on new hires by the MBA program that trained them. He talked more about the analysis and then paused. He looked at the Dean and began to explain that the results were not good for the managers hired from the university's MBA program.

In recent years a pattern had emerged and became clear over time. HR staff could predict with some accuracy the slowdown in promotions and performance for the university's MBAs as they reached three to five years with the company. The managers seemed to consistently stall at that point. Statistical analysis had been conducted, the staff reviewed about ten years of data and compared managers from various MBAs programs. The differences were striking. Graduates from other MBA programs typically advanced in the firm for over ten years to higher division executive positions. The VP reported that after re-checking the analysis, staff made a recommendation to discontinue recruiting from the university's MBA program. The VP reported that he took time to consider the analysis and recommendation. In the end, he said he had to agree, the data was clear. The purpose of the meeting was to inform the Dean the company would no longer recruit or hire MBA's from the university.

The Dean was not expecting this news, he was dismayed and shocked. He thanked the VP for the meeting and his clear explanation. He told the VP he would meet with faculty to address the matter and determine a plan with the hope the company would eventually consider hiring graduates from their MBA program again in the future.

The case somewhat dramatic, yet is an example of using recruiting metrics to decide on sources of new hires.

QUESTIONS TO ANSWER

1 Consider the firm's cost to recruit and hire the MBAs. The tradeoff is to hire graduates that tend to grow and develop for just 3 to 5 years versus other graduates that advance in the firm for 10 to 15 years.

 A Prepare a rough estimate of costs to send two recruiters to a campus: include airfare, lodging, meals & materials for 50 applicants. Assume recruiters travel from Chicago with two days at a campus in a somewhat distant state. Assume airline tickets at about $400 per person, lodging about $130 per person per night, meals about $40/day.

 B Prepare a rough estimate to fly 10 applicants to Chicago for two days of testing, interviews and dinners with two managers.

 C Prepare a rough estimate to train 10 new hires for one week with pay at $50,000 per week. See Table 5.1 on cost estimates to train new hires.

D Total the amounts in A, B and C, add a relocation allowance of $15, 000 to move each new hire and his or her three-person family: the value of maintaining metrics for recruiting decisions is equal to at least the total investment in recruiting + hiring.

Sample Materials: HR Design of Recruiting Metrics by Source of Applicants

Table 6.1   Recruiting Metrics to Evaluate Sources of Job Applicants Previously Hired

Statistics	Formulae	All Three Sources Totaled	Newspaper Ads	Online Job Boards	State Job Service Agency
# Accepted & Hired		200	95	75	30
# Initial Contacts		370	195	120	55
Total Job Offers Made		268	140	88	40
Total Days to Fill All Jobs: Initial contact to Hire date		11,600 Days	5,915	4,125	1,560
Total Cost to Hire All		$592,850	$401,375	$124,250	$67,225
Total Job Performance Appraisal Pts all hires, at 1-year post hire-Max =100/Hire		15,600	6,395	6,675	2,530
Total # of Quits of new hire group		90	51	27	12
RECRUITING RATIOS					
1 Selection Rate	# Hired / # Initial Contacts	200/370 = 54.1%	95/195 =48.7%		
2 Offers Accepted / Offers Made	# Accepted-Hired/ # Jobs Offered	200/268 = 74.6%	95/140 =67.9%		
3 Average Days to Fill Each Job Vacancy	Total # of Days / # Hired	11,600 / 200 = 58 Days	5,915/95 = 62 Days		
4 Average Cost per New Hire	Total Cost / # Hired	$592,850 / 200 = $2,964	$401,375/95 =$4,225		
5 Average Job Performance Appraisal Pts after 1st year per New Hire	Total Job Performance Pts / # Hired	15,600 / 200 = 78/100 Ps	6,395/95 =67.3/100 Pts		
6 Average Turnover Rate	# of Quits / # Hired	90 / 200 = 45%	51/95 = 53.7%		

Note: #s and ratios in chart are hypothetical. Results may be similar for some employers and not others.

HR Problem to Solve: Calculate Metrics for Two Sources & Identify Best Source of Three

QUESTIONS to ANSWER

1 Calculate metrics in Table 6.1 for the two sources in columns on the right, applicants found via Online Job Boards & State Job Service Agency. Enter ratios into chart.

Use formulae shown in the chart to calculate each metric.

See sample calculations in columns on the left: "Three sources totaled" & for "Newspaper ads."

2   What is the best overall source of job candidates in and explain why?

3   What is the second best overall source and explain why?

1st HR Design to Create: Prepare a Sample Chart of Employee Performance by Recruiting Source

Design a chart with hypothetical recruiting data for a list of employees for a job title you know well. Think about high versus low quality recruiting sources for applicants for that job title.

- o Recall Table 3.3 on legal issues in hiring with a row of data for each employee.
- o Imagine the data items the firm kept in the Case - Part B on recruiting metrics. They tracked data by employee by recruiting source for many years.
- o Instead of analyzing by manager as shown in Table 3.3, analyze employee performance results by recruiting source
- o The chart could have three columns for three different recruiting sources and several column to display employee performance, promotion, and attendance scores for eight or more employees per recruiting source. Design the hypothetical data with higher scores for new hires from a higher quality source and lower scores for hires from a lower quality source to demonstrate how real data might reveal important decision making information. The chart will show a manager how to collect and organize actual data to evaluate recruiting sources and ultimately help the firm hire higher performing employees.

2nd HR Design to Create: Prepare an Original Sample High Quality Job Ad

Research shows information rich job ads are more likely to attract applicants than low information ads (Allen, Mahto & Otondo, 2007). The lack of information in jobs ads often causes confusion. A key goal of job ads is to answer questions for applicants to make informed decisions on whether the job is suited to them or not.

- o -Choose a job title you know well and refer to the ONET website for job details (www.onetonline.org).

- o -Include detailed information on the following topics in your job ad. This data helps potential applicants decide if the job and the company fit with their job skills, preferences, values and more:
  - o Job Information: title, tasks, responsibilities, location, starting pay, job design, benefits, work setting, etc.
  - o Application Process Info: How, where and when (start & end date to accept applicants)
  - o Applicant Requirements: education, experience, knowledge, abilities
  - o Company values & culture: mission strategy, recognition, team vs individual work approach, creative vs structured setting, stable or changing operations, firm accomplishments, etc.
  - o Aesthetically pleasing presentation of information to attract applicants

3rd HR Design to Create: Prepare List of Sample Sources & Contact Info to Recruit Applicants

Smaller employers often are not aware of places to post ads to access excellent sources of job applicants. Select a job you know well and create a design with a detailed list of higher quality sources likely to attract qualified applicants.

Include the following categories of information in your design:
- o   Job Title as target vacancy to fill
- o   Type of Recruiting Source: print media, broadcast media, online job board, campus career websites, career fairs, social media, career field journals, industry associations, etc.
- o   Target applicant population: general population, specific career field, students, military veterans, etc.
- o   Contact information by source: names, address, phone, web URL, etc.
- o   Ad sizes, duration, cost options, etc.
- o   Type of Company information needed to place an ad
- o   Type of job Information to include (see items for information rich job ad in 2nd HR Design to Create)

{Intentionally Blank]

{Intentionally Blank]

Chapter 7 Select & Hire Job Candidates

Introduction with Cause and Effect Relationships

Employers use many methods to tests job candidates. The quality and validity of tests determine an employer's ability to use test scores to predict future job performance of candidates. Research has shown certain tests predict candidates' future job performance better than other tests. Valid tests to hire candidates include work sample tests, job knowledge tests, performance tests and structured interviews. For example, National Football League teams put college football players as potential draftees through a group of tests referred to as a "combine" (Heneman, Judge & Kammeyer-Mueller, 2012, pp 438). Each player's skills are tested along with strength, agility and intelligence. Some tests in an NFL combine operate as work samples. They mimic tasks and duties a player must perform on the field in an actual game. Employers are wise to conduct tests in a manner similar to the NFL. Test candidates' abilities to do actual job duties and tasks.

Hunter & Hunter (1984) conducted a meta-analysis and looked at many research studies on the validity of work sample tests across many occupations in many industries. They found an average correlation of .54 between work sample tests scores of candidates and corresponding job performance appraisal scores for those candidates after they were hired and worked for some time. Correlating a hiring test score and employee subsequent performance appraisal scores is a process to validate hiring tests. See Table 7.5 for sample data of hiring test scores and job performance scores. Data is hypothetical, yet the data is designed to represent results found in research studies.

The validity of each hiring test will be different for each firm due to different applicants, different implementation methods, etc. Each firm needs to verify the validity of hiring tests to predict future job performance for candidates they hire. Hiring test scores and job performance appraisals scores for new hires are entered to a database similar to information shown in Table 7.5. After data has been collected for at least 30 employees for a specific hiring test, statistical analysis via correlations can be conducted.

A mantra often heard from HR managers in hiring is, "Hire hard, and manage easy." Valid testing is a rigorous method to hire candidates. Future job performance is the outcome factor in the cause and effect relationship. It is easier to manage high performing employees versus poor performers.

High versus Low Quality HR Practices

In addition to work sample tests, research has shown other testing methods that predict future job performance scores well. Job knowledge tests had an average correlation to job performance scores of .41 (Hunter & Hunter, 1984), structured interviews, an average correlation of .51 (McDaniel, Schmidt & Mauer, 1994), IQ tests, an average correlation of .51 (Hunter, 1980) and conscientiousness tests, an average correlation to job performance scores of .31 (Ones, Viswesvaran, & Schmidt, 1993). Informal interviews are not considered a high quality method and serve best as a brief screening process. Think of a basketball, hockey or other sports team. Sports tryouts are types of work sample tests of specific skills of endurance, accuracy, athletic skills, etc. For many jobs, using valid methods can mean asking candidates to do a physical task to be observed by an expert. High quality methods also include the use of a fair rubric to assess each candidates' abilities. Hiring cashiers, servers, and chefs is similar to selecting players for a sports team. They must have the skills to do the work and to interact with customers. Role play tests with mock customers (current employees) in a work sample can test social interaction skills.

Case: Negligent Hiring & Screening Applicants to Identify Candidates for More Testing

One day senior managers at a large clinical care facility were urgently called to the President's conference room. The VP of Clinical Operations informed the group that moments ago an incident occurred in a triage area in the presence of a doctor and clinical staff treating an ill patient. A newly hired male Clinical Technician (CT) was in the group treating the patient. The CT had suddenly become very angry and brutally punched a nurse in the face. Security staff were onsite and quickly brought the tall and strong CT under control. Police officers arrived to arrest the Clinical Technician for assaulting the nurse. Her face was seriously bruised and she had lost a tooth. Clinical staff tended the nurse's injuries. How could this happen? Were other patients and staff safe? The firm had a reputation of excellent nursing care. The location was a suburban community with relatively low crime levels.

In the conference room, the President instructed the senior managers that he needed a quick decision on next steps. The police captain had called him to say State law enforcement records indicated the Clinical Technician had a prison record for multiple cases of violence against women. It was a shocking fact. Many females worked in the facility; all patients were vulnerable and many were female. How was this CT hired? Senior managers looked to the Director of HR. He apologized and admitted that criminal background checks were not a routine part of the screening process for new hires. He sheepishly admitted that HR needed to start doing that immediately. Members of the senior group were aghast. Could more incidents occur?

The president was dismayed, yet he needed the group to focus. He said, "We need to give the press a statement. We need to assure the public and our employees that we have a safe facility." "Yet, we have an injured nurse. Legal advisors have urged that we not admit to wrong doing to avoid large expenses from a potential law suit by the injured nurse." Hiring the CT was clearly an error of leadership. A few managers began to moan and expressed the desire to avoid large settlement costs. However, two voices spoke up with conviction. They advised the president to be honest, to apologize, and to take care of the injured nurse's needs from the incident.

QUESTION to ANSWER

1   What do you recommend the President say to the press?

2   How do you recommend the President and the senior managers respond to the injured nurse?

3   What follow up steps should HR staff take in regard to hiring new employees?

4   What other corrective actions might be helpful?

NOTE 1: Local laws regulate use of criminal background checks to make hiring decisions. Several states and municipalities limit criminal background checks to only those settings with a need based on business requirements (e.g. honesty of bank staff, executives), public safety or the presence of vulnerable persons.

NOTE 2: Companies often use experts to check criminal background and credit on job applicants. Numerous governmental units, agencies and others hold different pieces of data on these topics. Data on an individual can be conflicting due to errors by different entities. Experts try to verify accuracy as best they can.

Sample Materials: Screening New Hires in Settings with Vulnerable Persons

Applicant screening consists of initial steps in hiring to discuss application information with potential job candidates. This initial information helps identify applicants not suited well to the job due to lack of basic qualifications, poor fit with required work schedules, locations, travel requirements and more. It is important to eliminate applicants with a poor fit to avoid incurring needless candidate testing costs. Schools, clinical facilities, retirement settings and similar entities with vulnerable persons usually obtain signed forms from candidates to give the firm permission to do certain background checks including criminal records and more.

Table 7.1 Screening Checklist to Identify Potential Job Candidates in Settings with Vulnerable Persons

Phone or Informal Interview	Type of Questions	Screening Item
	Yes/No	1 Available to work job schedule?
	Yes / No	2 Available to work Job location?
	Yes / No	3 Able to do key physical job tasks, lifting, standing, etc.?
	Yes / No	4 Able to interact with vulnerable persons, children, sick people.
	Short answer	5 Any job related experience?
	Short answer	6 Any job related education, training?
	Short answer	7 Any job related certificates, license?
	Short answer	8 Any extracurricular activities?
	Short answer	9 Any experience working in teams?
	Short answer	10 Available for about one day to complete job tests?
Other Screening Checks	Yes / No	11 Able to provide letters of recommendation?
	Signed approval (a)	12 Willing to approve of reference checks with prior employers?
	Signed approval (a)	13 Willing to approve of criminal background check?
	Yes / No (b)	14 Willing to give finger prints?
	Signed approval (a)	15 Willing to approve of credit check?

(a) Best practices are to create approval forms for candidates to give permission to conduct specific screening checks with external parties. All signed approval forms should be kept in each candidate's file.

(b) Schools often collect finger prints from job candidates as part of criminal background check.

QUESTIONS to ANSWER

Think of a job title you know well. Imagine you are the hiring manager for a firm owned by your favorite uncle. You need to hire 10 people for this job. HR staff have recruited 40 qualified applicants.

Job Title to fill vacancies_____   Company Industry_____

1 Indicate screening items by number in Table 7.1, 3rd column that you would use in the hiring process_____

2 List any other items not in Table 7.1 that your feel should be in the screening process for this job title:

_____ _____ _____ _____ _____

Framework for Structured Behavioral Job Interview Questions with STAR Method
See Table 7.2
- Each question is structured to assess a specific & important job related skill.
- Rubric displays sample responses for each question for different quality levels of responses.
- Rubric shows sample high, average & poor quality responses via the STAR method to rate candidates.
- Unique sample responses by question helps interviewers use same criteria to rate candidates.
- Many companies use the STAR method to rate candidates in structured interviews (Carnol, 2015).
    - Situation, candidate describes the setting, context of past experience
    - Task, candidate describes what he/she needed to do or was asked to do
    - Action, candidate describes what he/she did
    - Results, candidate describes outcome of his or her action taken
- Goal: identify candidates with better answers, who responds in an organized and detailed manner.
- Managers & supervisors serve as subject matter experts (SMEs) to develop questions and rubrics.
- Aim is to assess key job skills with identical questions for each candidate, rate candidates fairly.

Valid & Predictive High Quality Interview Questions
- Behavioral structured interview questions shown in Table 7.2 focus on candidate past behaviors. Questions often start with a phrase such as "tell me about a time when you _ (did a job related task, had a problem) __, what did you do?
- Situational structured questions focus on hypothetical situations. Questions frequently begin with a phrase such as "imagine you are in a situation with a _ (job related problem) _describe what you would do. Questions focus on work situations candidates have not experienced.
- Research results: job related structured questions & rubrics are often valid to predict job performance.
    o High interview scores predict likely high future job performance scores
    o Low interview scores predict likely low future job performance scores.

AIM of Structured Interviews: Use Specific Criteria to Rate Candidates as Olympic Judges Rate Athletes
- Olympic judges hammer out items for rating rubrics prior to events to rate each athlete fairly.
- Use same criteria to rate each athlete's gymnastic or figure skating skills.
- Agree in advance on required moves, posture and composure of each athlete to measure performance.
- Tight array of scores for a given athlete indicate fair ratings by judges, such as between 9.0 and 9.3.
- Tight array of scores indicates judges are in agreement on performance, all used same criteria

Invalid Interview Questions / Poorly Designed Rubrics– do not predict future job performance
- Poor Questions with yes / no answers & Questions with short answers
- Use these questions in initial screening, see Table 7.1, assess availability, basic fit and more

    Poor Rating scales, brief & identical for all questions, such as Excellent, Average & Poor
- Cause interviewers to default to own criteria to define excellent, average and poor
- Interviewer criteria often not job related due to vague rating scale.
- Interviewers rate on different criteria such as likability; niceness, attractiveness (biased, not job skills)
- Cause arguments among interviewers on candidate ranking, each interviewer has very different scores

Sample Materials: Structured Behavioral Interview Questions & STAR Rubric – Past Behaviors

JOB TITLE: <u>Advanced Technology Assembly Technician</u>
JOB SKILL to MEASURE: Ability to maintain manufacturing protocols to meet product quality specifications

Table 7.2 Structured Behavioral Interview Questions & Rubric

1st Question	Tell me about a time when you felt pressured by someone to take short cuts in a task in a technical process. What did you do?
10 Pts Sample High Quality Response	
Situation	In college we often had team projects. We had a slacker on one team with a complex project. He was not completing his section, not in class, did not respond to our emails.
Task	I had to convince my team not to omit his section and hand in a weak paper. They were upset, yet we all wanted an A on the project.
Action	I urged the team to divide up his work and complete it for the team. We could inform the instructor. By each student doing extra work we could hand in a better paper.
Results	The team agreed to do the extra work. We talked to the teacher, he seemed to know about the slacker. We earned an A on the project.
5 Points Average	
Task	I had to convince teammates in college not to hand in a weak paper due to a slacker who did not complete his sections.
Results	Other team members did the slacker's sections and we earned an A on the project.
-0- Points Poor	
Wrong Answer	Short cuts can save time so I usually take them, if I can see steps to leave out.

JOB SKILL to MEASURE: Skill and initiative to search for technical solutions to solve complex problems.

2nd Question	Tell me about a time when you had to answer a technical question, but you did not immediately have an answer. What did you do?
10 Pts Sample High Quality Response	
Situation	I was a club officer for my major in college. I heard about a certification test we could take as a credential for our resumes. Other club members were unsure. We did not know if we were eligible, what the test was, and when to take it.
Task	I searched for information to share with members to convince them to talk to professionals to learn more and to form study groups to prepare for the test.
Action	I found most details online on eligibility, study materials, and where to sign up to take the test. Professionals told me the credential was important for our careers
Results	I shared the Information with club members. They agreed to form a study group to prepare. Nearly all of us passed the test and became certified.
5 Points Average	
Situation	I found out we could take a test to be certified for our major in college.
Results	A group of us studied together and nearly all of us passed and became certified.
Zero Pts Poor Quality	
Wrong Answer	When I do not know an answer I usually refer the question to a supervisor.

1st HR Design to Create: Prepare Original Sample Structured Interview Questions for a Job Title

Job Title_____
1st JOB SKILL TO MEASURE:_____

1st Question

High Quality Sample Response
        Situation

            Task

            Action

            Results

Average Sample Response
        Situation or Task or Action

            Result

Poor Quality Sample Response

            Wrong answer

2ND JOB SKILL TO MEASURE:_____
2nd Question & Rubric based on STAR approach

High Quality Sample Response
        Situation

            Task

            Action

            Results

Average Sample Response
        Situation or Task or Action

            Result

Poor Quality Sample Response

            Wrong answer

[Intentionally Blank]

Sample Materials: HR Design on Work Sample Test Protocol

Table 7.3 Work Sample Tests for Receptionist / Typist in Accounting Firm

Key Information Protocol	Details by Job Title
1 Job Title & Industry	Receptionist / Typist in Accounting Firm
2 Describe Test Setting	Back office set up as mock reception area with chairs for mock clients
3 Skills / Abilities to Test	Typing speed-accuracy/grammar-spelling/computer skills, interaction skills
4 Materials for Test	Desk, chairs & functioning equipment computer & phone
5 Activities Candidate to Perform	A Skills Independent of Others
	i Type letter by listening to a tape of a manager's mock recorded letter
	ii Correct spelling, grammar errors in mock letter
	iii Use computer, Microsoft Office, Email, Phone system, Voice mail
	B Interaction Skills
	i Mock client (current employee actor) arrive a day early for appointment
	ii Mock accountant (current employee actor) possibly meet early client
	Iii Observer to rate candidate using rubric
6 Briefing Topics Pre Training	A Two to four hours to learn equipment, practice
	B Work values: Cooperate, courteous, helpful, initiative-solve problem
	C Intro to computer, email
	D Intro to phone system

Table 7.4 Rubric to Rate Receptionist Candidate Performance

Work Sample Test	Criteria	Lowest Rating	Low-Avg.	Avg.	Avg. -High	Highest Rating
15 minute Typing Test	WPM*	50 or less: 4 Pts	75: 8 Pts	100: 12	125: 16 Pts	150: 20 Pts
15 Minute Typing Test	Errors	10 or more: 4 Pts	7: 8 Pts	5: 12 Pts	2: 16 Pts	Zero: 20 Pts
Letter Spell/ Grammar	Errors	12 or more: 4 Pts	7: 8 Pts	5: 12 Pts	2: 16 Pts	Zero: 20 Pts
Email: compose, attach, Reply, move, forward	# Tasks Done Well	1 Task: 2 Pts	2: 4 Pts	3: 6 Pts	4: 8 Pts	5: 10 Pts
Word: compose, copy, Save, create folder, file	# Tasks Done Well	1 Task: 2 Pts	2: 4 Pts	3: 6 Pts	4: 8 Pts	5: 10 Pts
Excel: enter, insert, layout Design, format	# Tasks Done Well	1 Task: 2 Pts	2: 4 Pts	3: 6 Pts	4: 8 Pts	5: 10 Pts
Phone: call, reply, leave & receive voice mail, forward	# Tasks Done Well	1 Task: 2 Pts	2: 4 Pts	3: 6 Pts	4: 8 Pts	5: 10 Pts
Role Play: Client arrives a day early						
Prompt to greet client						2 Pt
Interpret appointment log						4 Pts
Identify client problem						2 Pts
Courteous-respect client						10
Courteous-accountant						8
Offer client time to meet						8
Initiative, solve problem						6
MAX Points: All Tests						140 Points

*WPM: Words typed per minute

2nd HR Design to Create: Prepare a Work Sample Test Protocol

Think of a job you know well or one assigned to you for this task
Work Sample Protocol

1   Job Title: _____   Industry: _____

2   Describe Test Setting:

3   Skills or Abilities to Test:

4   Materials or Props for Test:

5   Activities each Candidate to Perform:

6   Briefing topics & Pre-Training for Candidate

7   RUBRIC to Rate Each Candidate's Performance:

List of Tasks/Actions Candidate to Complete	Criteria	Lowest Rating	Low-Avg.	Average	Avg.-High	Highest Rating
1						
2						
3						
4						
5						
6						
7						
8						
9						
10						

Maximum Possible Points:

Table 7.5   Data on Hiring Test Scores and Job Performance Scores after Hire

Employee Name	Work Sample	Conscien- tiousness	Job Knowledge	Structured Interview	6 month Appraisal	12 month Appraisal	18 month Appraisal	24 month Appraisal	Average Appraisal
Hired 2-yrs ago	Max 100	Max 20	Max 100	Max 30	Max 30	Max 30	Max 30	Max 30	Max 30
1	78	14	75	28	18	22	24	24	21.75
2	70	15	65	22	18	20	21	21	20.25
3	60	11	58	18	15	16	19	19	17.75
4	85	13	73	26	19	24	26	26	24
5	78	11	62	27	18	22	24	24	22.25
6	48	7	68	12	11	14	15	15	14.25
7	80	16	75	21	26	25	27	27	25.5
8	58	13	55	20	14	16	18	18	17
9	45	11	60	18	12	15	18	18	15.25
10	30	9	40	8	8	10	11	11	10.5
11	.0	7	43	9	8	9	12	12	10.75
12	38	9	42	14	10	12	12	12	12
13	42	7	45	18	11	13	15	15	13.75
14	85	15	82	28	18	20	23	23	21.25
15	92	14	88	27	24	25	24	24	24.75
16	68	16	82	25	19	21	22	22	21.25
17	71	12	66	24	18	20	22	22	20.75
18	76	15	54	26	19	21	22	22	21.75
19	81	14	85	25	19	22	23	23	22.25
20	55	13	49	12	15	17	19	19	17.25
21	60	12	45	19	16	18	21	21	19.75
22	68	11	79	23	14	15	20	20	17
23	62	14	61	21	26	24	25	25	25.5
24	48	10	47	13	13	16	21	21	17.75
25	53	12	48	22	18	21	22	22	21
26	55	15	63	24	17	20	20	20	20.25
27	76	6	35	28	22	24	28	28	24.75
28	82	16	90	27	18	20	19	19	19.75
29	51	18	55	19	19	22	22	22	21.5
30	73	14	75	20	23	28	26	26	25.25
31	52	5	63	15	20	25	22	22	22.75
32	41	7	76	10	28	29	25	25	26.5
33	62	19	76	24	18	19	16	16	18.75
34	88	4	73	28	15	15	21	21	18.5
Correlate with Avg. Appraisal	r = .64	r = .24	r = .47	r = .49					

A general rule for hiring is: a single test cannot be the silver bullet to predict job performance for any job title (Heneman, Judge & Kammeyer-Mueller, 2012). Each job title has different job tasks and duties that require different tests. Firms are advised to use multiple valid tests as predictors to assess candidates. This requires a method to combine the multiple tests scores to rank candidates. Two methods are described here.

The multiple hurdles test means candidates must achieve a minimum score on each test before being eligible to take the next test (Mathis & Jackson, 2011). When a candidate fails one test they fall out of contention as a job candidate. This method is most often used for roles with high impact decision making (e.g. executives) or jobs with life and death consequences such as fire fighters, EMT, paratroopers, etc. An EMT needs numerous lifesaving skills to be qualified. A candidate can't fail in cardiac pulmonary resuscitation (CPR) and qualify as an EMT.

The compensatory method is a 2nd approach to assess multiple test scores. Here all points are added together (Mathis & Jackson, 2011). Scores may be weighted. The weighted scores are summed to arrive at a total score by candidate. Candidates with higher scores are rated highest. Most firms set a minimum required overall total score for candidates. This says that scoring high in one test can make up for or COMPENSATE for a low score in another test. Most students' final course grades in college are determined in this manner.

Part A: COMPENSATORY METHOD to combine multiple test scores of job candidates
Steps To Do:
1   See points entered for employee #1. His score for job knowledge is 46, worth 10 points
2   Determine the points each candidate earned in each test
3   Add each candidates total points, enter total in 6th column
4   <u>Minimum required Total Points to be eligible</u> for a formal interview is <u>28 Points.</u>
5   Rank eligible candidates, best score equals #1 rank, enter rank in 7th column

1 Employee #	2 Job Knowledge Max Points = 50	3 Work Sample Max Points = 100	4 Conscientiousness Max Points = 70	5 Team Skills Role Play Max Points = 50	6 Total Points	7 Rank if Eligible
	45-50: 10 Pts	90-100: 10 Pts	63-70: 10 Pts	45-50: 10 Pts	Max = 40	
	40-44: 8 Pts	80-89: 8 Pts	56-62: 8 Pts	40-44: 8 Pts		
	35-39: 7 Pts	70-79: 7 Pts	49-55: 7 Pts	35-39: 7 Pts		
	30-34: 6 Pts	60-69: 6 Pts	42-48: 6 Pts	30-34: 6 Pts		
	Less than 30: -0-	Less than 60: -0-	Less than 42: -0-	Less than 30: -0-		
1	46—10 Pts	82—8 Pts	54—7 Pts	43—8 Pts	33 Pts	
2	40	90	50	46		
3	32	63	42	34		
4	39	75	48	39		
5	33	58	50	42		
6	40	95	46	38		
7	43	86	63	47		
8	39	71	51	36		

Problem continues on next page.

Part B   MULTIPLE HURDLES METHOD to combine multiple test scores of job candidates
Steps to Do:

1. Review each column, did any fail to meet the minimum? See 2nd column, #4 at 75 is below minimum.
2. Mark "OUT" for scores below minimum. Anyone failing is automatically OUT, regardless of other scores
3. For candidates who meet all minimum required scores, indicate yes in column 6, sum scores in column 7.
4. See scores for #1, he met all minimums and the sum of his scores is 350.
5. Indicate Rank of the candidates who meet all minimum required scores in column 8.

1 Employee #	2 Work Sample Max = 100	3 Case Study Max = 100	4 Physical Endurance Max = 100	5 Job Knowledge Max = 100	6 Eligible Yes / No	7 Sum of Scores	8 Rank
	Minimum Required: 85	Min. Req. 80	Min. Req. 90	Min. Req. 80			
1	88	87	90	85	YES	350	
2	90	82	91	86			
3	86	93	92	89			
4	78 OUT	82 OUT in 1st test	80 OUT in 1st test	75 OUT in 1st test	NO	OUT	
5	85	83	93	81			
6	91	94	95	90			
7	74	79	83	68			
8	83	80	76	78			
9	96	95	91	87			
10	89	84	88	76			

[Intentionally Blank]

Chapter 8 Training Employees

Introduction with Cause and Effect Relationships

Training is a critical component of business operations. The 2014 industry report by the Association for Talent Development reported that average annual spending per employee for training in the U.S. was $1,208 in 2013; and average annual number of learning hours per employee was 31.5 hours (Miller, 2014). This amounts to billions of dollars spent by employers across the U.S. The data was based on input from 340 organizations in a variety of company sizes and industries. These amounts were similar to and slightly higher than 2012 averages.

Why do companies invest in employee training? Recent reports by HR Magazine and the American Association for Training and Development (ASTD) surveyed hundreds of companies in different industries and found that those with more comprehensive investment in training experienced an average of 24% higher profit margins than companies with lower expenditures in training (Riskalla, 2015). Research involving quasi-experimental field studies report a number of beneficial outcomes from specific training programs. For example, orientation programs for new hires with a focus on company values, history, goals and people showed significantly higher commitment to the organization for employees who attended the training compared to others who did not (Klein & Weaver, 2000). Self-management training for lower performing insurance sales persons resulted in increases in sales revenue, policies sold and self-efficacy of trainees more than double the results for similar salespersons in a control group without the training (Frayne & Geringer, 2000). Training on verbal self-guidance for teams found trainees had significantly higher team performance and team-efficacy compared to a control group of teams without the training (Brown, 2003).

Training programs cover many topics on both hard job skills and soft social interactional skills. Employees unprepared to do a job can create problems and high costs for a firm. Employers need to monitor training needs as products, technology and other changes occur in an organization. Some companies have transformed training expertise to new sources of revenue as trainers also give instruction to customers for effective use of products. Companies have hired Chief Learning Officers (Mathis & Jackson, 2011) at the executive level to bring training topics to the Board of Directors level to include training as part of strategic decision making.

High versus Low Quality HR Practices

Quality of training depends on more than dollars spent per year. High quality training involves careful planning and assessment of employee training needs. Learners must be prepared for technical content. For example, if employees have generally worked in a low technology environment and need to migrate to a technical way to work, they likely need a stepwise training process. Some employees would likely need introductions on basic computer skills before learning how to use complex software systems. Trainers must also be expert in instructional material. For example, time and expense is often wasted when untrained supervisors who are reluctant to be a trainer are put in charge of instruction. Training delivery options include instructor led classrooms, on-the job training, job shadowing, individual online learning and other formats. Delivery must be calibrated to the content aimed at learners. For example, basic concepts may be taught through self-instruction via e-training. As concepts increase in complexity, delivery methods must be ramped up to help learners. For example, training might include an instructor, exercises, time to practice, feedback and skill testing. More in depth approaches for complex material give employees guidance and time to perform new skills. In summary, many training dimensions must be considered to develop excellent programs: needs of learners, skills of trainers, and materials, fit of delivery methods, and training time and setting. Finally, companies need to assess training outcomes to assure dollars spent on training are wise investments to help improve organizational outcomes (Mathis & Jackson, 2011).

Sample Materials: HR Design on Orientation Training for New Employees

Researchers found new employees had higher commitment to the organizations two and a half months after orientation training was completed compared to new employees who did not attend the training. Orientation training focused on company history (traditions, stories, ceremonies, etc.), goals and values (mission, goals and values) and the structure and people in the organization. The research involved 116 non-faculty new employees in an education organization. Employees held a variety of different job titles (Klein & Weaver, 2000)

SAMPLE ORIENTATION TRAINING PLAN: All Job Titles
Many plan items are based the training process described in the research study.

Structure:
- 3 hours of training
- Two experienced HR staff trainers, maximum of 30 new employees per training session
- Invitations to send: three and one week notice to new employees & their supervisors

Materials:
- 3-ring binders per learner - information on history, traditions, mission, structure
- Video welcome from organization leader, President and others
- Games with prizes to get acquainted and learn info on key topics in binders
- Welcome gifts and snacks, certificates of completion
- Video or slides on mission, history, terms & common acronyms used, structure
- Photographer for group shot upon completion
- Tests, surveys to assess learner retention and satisfaction with training

Methods:
- Instructor lectures and guided discussion
- Group activities, games, competitions on information learned

Agenda of Topics to Discuss & Materials in Binder for Each Attendee:
- Notes on Presidents video welcome
- Message to new employees, how they can be key contributors to organizational success
- Mission, purpose, aims and future impact of company
- History, noteworthy employees, leaders, creative output, growth over time,
- Organization founding – date, location, founding group,
- Recognition & Achievements of Organization – Top quality awards, community service
- Employee Recognition Programs & Activities:
  - Employee achievements & success awards
  - 5 – 10 – 15+ length of service awards,
  - Summer picnic with family games & competitions;
  - Winter party with gifts
- Facts & Figures – total employees, gross revenue & growth, market area
- Highlights of company calendar, events, celebrations
- Recent quarterly organizational newsletter to all employees
- Acronyms, jargon and language unique to industry, company and jobs
- Organizational chart with reporting relationships
- Workplace principles, work habits, dress, attendance, communication,
- Q & A time for attendees

Plan continues on next page.

Sample Invitation-Flyer: Send three weeks and one week in advance to new employees & supervisors

(Company Logo)

EVENT: NEW EMPLOYEE ORIENTATION – Informative & Fun

TO: All New Employees, started work within 60 days of session
FROM: Human Resource Department

Photo of past groups smiling, certificates, fun time

Purpose: Welcome to Sage Tree University!
                       Orientation Training, Snacks, Games, Prizes, Gifts
                       Information binder for you, photos, newsletter, more
                       Meet other new employees
                       Talk to HR Representatives, time for Q & A

Location: HR Classroom, 301, 3rd Floor
Dates: 2nd Wednesday monthly
Time: 9 am to Noon
Dress: Business Professional
Registration: Advance registration, confirm acceptance by email
Attendees: Limited to a maximum of 30 persons per session
Contact: Phone: xxx-xxxx; Email: hrtrainers@sagetreeu.org
Website: www.sagetreesuniv.org/train see full agenda, more

Sample Materials: HR Design on Self-Management Training-Sales & Customer Service Reps

Researchers found insurance sales persons had higher job performance in total sales, number of policies sold and also in personal self-efficacy, all double on average compared to similar sales persons who did not attend the training. Training consisted of instructor-led training on self-management techniques. Trainees were 60 lower performing life insurance sales persons with half receiving the training and the other half received general organizational updates as the control group. The results indicated improvement in 6 months after training and also continued performance gains in the 12 months after training. Training consisted of self-assessment, self-setting goals, self-monitoring and self-evaluations and performance tracking. To develop training materials, managers identified behaviors that inhibited performance of the sales persons. Case materials were developed based on manager input. Employees in the control group did not initially receive training, but were later trained in the same techniques with similar favorable improvements in performance measures (Frayne & Geringer, 2000).

SAMPLE TRAINING PLAN on Self-Management Principles: Sales & Customer Service Reps
Many plan items are based on the training process described in the research study.

Structure:
- Eight hours of traditional classroom training,
- Four sessions, two hours per week for four weeks
- Two instructors, expert in goal setting and other management concepts.
- Maximum of 15 trainees per instructor
- Invitations to send: eight & four weeks before to lower performers and their supervisors.
- Collect information in advance from managers on behaviors that inhibit success
- Develop cases from information collected in advance

Materials:
- Binder of slides to take notes on lectures
- Cases
- Instructions for role play exercises
- Wrap up test, surveys to assess learning outcomes and training satisfaction
- Certificates of Completion & Snacks

Teaching Methods:
- Lectures cover one to two topics per week
- Homework to learn self-management concepts each week
- Cases on bad habits and how self-management principles can improve job performance
- Group discussion on cases
- Role play to practice applying principles, interact with mock clients, critique behavior

Agenda of Topics on Self-Management to Discuss:
- 1st Session: Self-assessments – systematically collect data on self on behaviors to change
- 2nd Session: Goal setting – individual short & long term behavior objectives to improve performance
- 3rd Session: -Self-monitoring – maintain records of goals to use in self-assessments
        -Self-evaluation – use self-set rewards & punishment as incentives for goals
- 4th Session -Written contract – self-agreement on behavior changes & goals
        -Maintenance & relapse prevention–identify high risk situations and behaviors

Plan continues on next page

Sample Tracking Chart to Monitor Self-Management Goals & Behaviors

Table 8.1 Tracking Chart on Self-Management Progress for Sales Person or Customer Service Representative

My Name: Date began this cycle:

Week	1st Goal	2nd Goal	3rd Goal	4th Goal	1st Behavior	2nd Behavior	3rd Behavior	4th Behavior	Assess
Week 1									
Week 2									
Week 3									
Week 4									
Month Total									
Week 5									
Week 6									
Week 7									
Week 8									
Month Total									
Define:	1st Goal								
	2nd Goal								
	3rd Goal								
	4th Goal								
Define:	1st Behavior								
	2nd Behavior								
	3rd Behavior								
	4th Behavior								

Scoring Legend: 1-Failed Goal; 2-Met Partial Goal; 3-Met full Goal; 4-Maintain Goal; 5-Exceed Goal
1-Failed new behavior; 2-partial behavior done; 3-new behavior success;
4-maintain new behavior; 5- Exceed new behavior

Researchers conducted a quasi-experimental study with 42 teams of college students on VSG techniques (Brown, 2003). Half the teams received training in VSG, the other half were the control groups and were coached on general teamwork concepts. Teams had to solve complex cases of poor quality HR practices in a firm and to recommend solutions for improve HR practices. HR issues addressed pay and appraisal systems. Team papers were graded by teaching assistants (TAs) who were unaware of the research study. A second group of TAs re-graded papers to assure consistency in applying the rubric. Team scores for the two sets of TAs were 90% correlated and assured scores were not biased. Results showed that teams with VSG training had higher scores compared to teams without VSG training. The training fostered favorable team interactions and members had higher team efficacy in a post study survey; they were more confident the team could achieve team goals.

SAMPLE TRAINING PLAN on Verbal Self Guidance for Work Teams
Many plan items are based on the training described in the research study.

Structure:
- One 90 minute session of classroom training, maximum of 30 trainees per instructor
- One instructor expert in VSG and NNP (Negative, Neutral, Positive statements in teams)
- Notify team members of team training session one month ahead of project start.

Materials:
- Binder of slides to take notes on lectures
- NNP handout of sample statements for team members to listen for in team interactions
- Instructions for role play exercises
- Wrap up test, surveys to assess learning outcomes and training satisfaction
- Certificates of Completion & Snacks

Teaching Methods:
- Lectures on team mission-goals; NNP Statements; Behavioral Observation Scale
- Group discussion of NNP statements, share examples of statements in past teams
- Role play practice in teams to apply NNP principles, interact, critique behavior

Agenda of Topics to Discuss
Team mission statements: Each team prepare mission statement, goals & strategy to do the work
Importance of teamwork and team skills
- Cooperate, support and coach each other on attitudes and effort to do a great job
- Plan at start of each phase: outline steps, tasks, group to clarify any member questions
- Check in for all to be on board with process, how to achieve success & great results

Role of positive versus negative language:
- Positives statements in teams tend to inspire, increase energy level.
- Negatives statements tend to deflate; detract attention to do a great job.

NNP Method: listen for Negatives, ask Neutral questions, and convert Negatives to Positives
- <u>Negatives, samples comments</u>: "<u>Can't d</u>o project," "<u>Never</u> finish on time," "<u>No way</u> to do the work"
- <u>Neutral</u> questions, samples to ask: "<u>What skills</u> could we use for this?" "<u>How did</u> we solve it before?" "<u>What </u>inhibits us?" "<u>What strategy</u> will help us do well?"
- <u>Positives,</u> samples to convert negatives: "<u>We can</u> do this with a plan. <u>We will finish</u> on time with a schedule. "<u>We can focus</u> on our goals and a strategy." "<u>We can</u> be successful!"
- Behavioral Observation Scale explained for each member to monitor self, and to confidentially complete on each other after project completed.

Plan continues on next page

Behavioral Observation Scale (BOS) for Team Members to Monitor Self
May also be used by Teammates to Confidentially Rate Individual Teammates after Project Completed

My Name_____   Name of Teammate Rated below_____

Rating Score to Use:
1   Strongly Disagree
2   Disagree Somewhat
3   Neutral
4   Agree Somewhat
5   Strongly Agree

Instruction: Think of the teammate named above to rate and answer the questions below to rate that teammate on the list of statements. The teammate:

Helped the group come to agreement on different issues	1	2	3	4	5
Explained in detail his or her ideas or position on an issue	1	2	3	4	5
Helped focus the group on the task	1	2	3	4	5
Actively listened to others' viewpoints without judging	1	2	3	4	5
Sought input of all members	1	2	3	4	5
Helped resolve conflicts among team members	1	2	3	4	5
Actively participated in team discussions	1	2	3	4	5
Was courteous with team members	1	2	3	4	5
Assertively defended his or her viewpoints, rather than giving in or being stubborn	1	2	3	4	5

NOTE: The above scale was tested to be valid and reliable by researchers as reported in:
    Brown, T.C. & Latham, G.P. 2002. The effectiveness of behavioral outcome goals, learning goals and urging people to do their best on an individual's teamwork behavior in a group problem-solving task. *Canadian Journal of Behavioral Science,* 34(4): 276-285.

Think of a job you know well and design a plan to give clear guidance on how to conduct OJT for employees. Design the plan for a supervisor who knows the job and tasks well, but often does not prepare well for training sessions. The lack of planning can cause new employees to receive inconsistent OJT from supervisors. Unfortunately, new employees may be unprepared to do required job tasks.

The plan should include the following sections of information for the training:
- Structure
- Materials
- Teaching Methods
- Topics to Discuss

OJT is generally done in the work setting with actual work equipment and materials. Teaching methods should include an introduction to put learners at ease and to inquire about their knowledge of the job, tasks, equipment, etc. OJT usually involves a detailed demonstration with explanations about each step; why each step is important, and who is impacted by the quality of how each step is completed. A detailed explanation and demonstration highlights the significance of each job task. This helps employees gain a sense of meaningfulness and responsibility that can be motivating as previously discussed in materials on job designs and the Job Characteristics Model.

Chapter 9 Appraise Employee Job Performance

Introduction with Cause and Effect Relationships

Employee job performance appraisals are an important, yet challenging area of HR. The fairness of performance ratings can influence employee motivation, attitudes, turnover and more. The most effective appraisal materials are specific and focused on job related duties. Forms associated with the better methods usually display detailed examples of different performance levels: high, average and poor for specific job tasks. High quality appraisal systems include written job performance standards for important job duties. Work standards should be given to employees shortly after they are hired (Schrader & Steiner, 1996). Unfortunately, performance standards are sometimes absent and employees may not have a job description; they may not know what is expected of them.

Performance management systems are made up of a series of interconnected activities including setting performance standards and measuring, evaluating and giving feedback to employees on job performance. This process is necessary for business success, to motivate and reward employees (Mathis & Jackson, 2011). The performance appraisal process has two primary dimensions: to measure employee performance and to communicate results to each employee. Several formats used in performance appraisals unfortunately can lead supervisors and managers to give biased appraisal scores. Bias stems from general and non-specific rating methods with measurement scales consisting of vague anchors. For example, terms on a rating form such as "outstanding, average and poor" are vague and lack definition. When this occurs in a work setting, each manager tends to interpret and judge employee performance differently based on his or her interpretation of the undefined scales. Some managers may actually rate employees based on likability or physical appearance. Some managers may tend to rate all employees similarly, such as rating all employees average or low. This can be a strategy by a manager to avoid arguments with employees who are in a single job title. For example, discussions on manager rating tendencies can be overhead on coffee breaks or in the cafeteria. In a larger organization a few managers had reputations for being tough raters on all their employees. Other managers were known to rate everyone in their work units average regardless of actual employee performance. Alternatively, rating methods with relevant and measurable job standards and detailed criteria tend to result in scores based on actual employee job performance.

High versus Low Quality HR Practices

The quality of a manager's job performance appraisal ratings depends on a number of factors. Training for managers on how to give fair appraisals is important. The rating criteria contained in rating forms are also key to the process (Jelley, Goffin, Powell, & Heneman, 2012). Organizations may focus on different types of appraisal information including employee traits, behaviors or results. The quality of each type of information depends on how it is applied and how well it relates to specific job tasks and duties. Higher quality appraisal methods tend to be based on specific performance criteria (Jelley & Goffin, 2001). Higher quality goals are supported by data tracking methods to build awareness on average performance of a work group over time. Also, clear statements on minimum acceptable work levels for key job tasks help build high quality performance appraisal processes. The sample materials for employee performance appraisals shown below are interrelated and focus on a single job title.

Sample Materials: HR Design of Job Duties Mapped to Work Standards & Goals

Current, accurate and detailed job descriptions form the basis to develop work standards. Mapping job tasks and duties in the job description to work standards can give supervisors and employees a basis to understand work standards. The mapping approach helps reduce bias in the rating process. Also, when employee job performance is tracked on a daily or weekly basis, bias in ratings is less likely. The data serves as evidence of actual performance.

Sample Map of Job Tasks & Duties to Potential Work Standards or Goal Items

Manufacturing Co. Inc.

JOB DESCRIPTION

JOB TITLE: Shipping, Receiving and Traffic Clerk
DEPARTMENT: Purchasing, Receiving and Shipping   OVERTIME STATUS: Non exempt
SUPERVISOR JOB TITLE: Shipping Supervisor   WORK CLASS: Operations

Summary Statement: Verify, maintain records on incoming and outgoing shipments. Prepare items for shipment. Duties include assembling, addressing, stamping, and shipping merchandise and materials; receiving, unpacking, verifying and recording incoming merchandise and materials; and arranging for transportation of products.

POTENTIAL ITEMS FOR JOB
STANDARDS OR WORK GOALS

ESSENTIAL JOB DUTIES:

- Examine shipment contents, verify accuracy.   1. Accurate orders
- Record shipment data: weight, charges, damages for permanent files.   2. Meet shipping targets
- Prepare work orders, bills of lading, or shipping orders, to route materials. 3. Meet receiving targets
- Confer with vendor representatives to rectify problems.   4. Maintain driver relations
- Pack and deliver materials using tools, postage meter.   5. Accurate computations
- Deliver or route materials to departments via hand truck or sorting bins. 6. Load / unload / deliver
- Requisition and store shipping materials and supplies to maintain inventory of stock.
- Determine shipping methods, routes, or rates for materials to be shipped.
- Compute expense amounts for shipping, storage and other charges using a price list.

KNOWLEDGE, SKILLS & ABILITIES

- Clerical, processing, customer service and personal services
- Communication, coordination, decision making   7. Concern for others, helpful
- Manual dexterity, visual acuity, lift over 50 lbs., extensive standing   8. Critical thinking
- Anticipate, identify, resolve problems   9. Maintain energy, stamina
- Organize, plan and process information and materials

WORK CONDITIONS, VALUES & PERSONAL STYLE

- Crew members, cooperative, adaptable, kind   10. Team skills
- Safe procedures with tools, equipment, lifting etc.   11. Safety
- Honesty   12. Integrity

Sample Materials: HR Design of Work Standards

Table 9.1 Work Standards per Employee: Shipping, Receiving and Traffic Clerk

JOB TITLE: Shipping, Receiving and Traffic Clerk, Regional Distribution Facility
DEPARTMENT: Purchasing, Receiving and Shipping   OVERTIME STATUS: Non exempt
SUPERVISOR JOB TITLE: Shipping Supervisor   WORK CLASS: Operations

Tasks & Behaviors	Prior Year Work Group Average per Day & New Work Standard	Prior Year Week Average & New Standard	Target per Day Improve prior Year Average By 20%	Target per Week
1 Score on data entry accuracy, orders & data to system [a]	Not applicable	4.0	Not applicable	4.5
2 Meet Shipping Targets	3 Shipments	15	4 shipments	20
3 Meet Receiving Targets	6 Receipts	30	7 Receipts	35
4 Score on driver relations [b]	Not applicable	3.5	Not applicable	4.2
5 Score on Computations [a]	Not applicable	3.2	Not applicable	3.8
6 Load / Unload / Deliver	Minutes drivers wait for unloads / loads	8 min. unload / 35 min. load	Minutes drivers wait for unloads / loads	7 min./ 30 min.
7 Concern for others, helpful [b]	Not applicable	3.8	Not applicable	4.4
8 Critical thinking [b]	Not applicable	4.1	Not applicable	4.8
9 Energy, stamina [b]	Not applicable	3.9	Not applicable	4.3
10 Team skills: cooperate [b]	Not applicable	3.6	Not applicable	4.2
11 Safe procedures	Not applicable	4.3	Not applicable	4.8
12 Integrity- honesty [b]	Not applicable	4.2	Not applicable	4.8

a. Based on audit of errors by week, with rating from 1 = Poor to 5 = Excellent.
b. Based on periodic survey of supervisors, peers, internal & external customers or drivers, with rating from 1 = Poor to 5 = Excellent.

Data Tracked by HRIS for each department and each employee, to give feedback and performance appraisals.

Sample Materials: HR Design of Individual Employee Performance Appraisal

Table 9.2 Performance Appraisal Form for Individual Employee

JOB TITLE: Shipping, Receiving and Traffic Clerk
Scores based on manager review of employee results in database.
DEPARTMENT: Purchasing, Receiving and Shipping   Employee Name: Normal Norm

Tasks & Behaviors	Below Work Standard 1	Meet Work Standard 2	Above Work Standard 3	Exceeds Targets Well Beyond Standard 4
1 Accurately Process Orders & log data to system			X	
2 Meet Shipping Targets			X	
3 Meet Receiving Targets				X
4 Maintain driver relations		X		
5 Accurate Computations			X	
6 Load / Unload / Deliver			X	
7 Concern for others, helpful				X
8 Critical thinking		X		
9 Maintain energy, stamina				X
10 Team skills: cooperate, kind			X	
11 Safe procedures			X	
12 Integrity- honesty			X	

Maximum potential score: 12 x 4 = 48

Overall Performance Appraisal Rating ___ Savvy Steve: 37/48 = 77.1%

HR Design to Create: Prepare Sample Performance Appraisal Materials

Think of a job you know well

Find key job duties for the job description at ONET www.onetonline.org

Prepare a Map of Job Duties in the Job Description to Potential Work Standards

Prepare a Set of Detailed Work Standards by Key Job Duties for the Job Title

Prepare s Sample Appraisal Rating Sheet for a Hypothetical Employee

[Intentionally Blank]

Chapter 10 Compensate Employees

Introduction with Cause and Effect Relationships

Organizations need strong pay structures for several reasons, three important considerations are:
- To assure wages are fair to motivate employees.
- To assure policies are fair to comply with the laws and avoid costly lawsuits.
- To control budgets for financial success

Market wages are key inputs to setting employee wages and developing wage budgets. The idea of "market wages" refers to average wages paid to persons in a specific job title in a certain geographic region. For example, last year's market wage rate for an accountant in a suburban region tended to be less than the average pay for similar accountants in a metropolitan area. The cost of living tends to be reflected in market wage rates. Exceptions to this general pattern might be a labor shortage for a job title. It can cause a spike in wage levels for the job title or career field due to greater job openings versus job seekers. Business activity also impacts market wage levels. For example, plant closings can result in many job seekers but few job openings in a region. An excess supply of labor in the form of job seekers tends to deflate market wage rates in a geographic area (Martocchio, 2013).

Market wage rates by job title are available on many websites. For example, ONET, www.onetonline.org, was developed by the U.S. Dept. of Labor to provide market wages by job title and by state for employers, job seekers, and others. Job services agencies in each state are a source of wage data. The agencies confidentially survey employers in the respective states on actual past wages paid to persons by job title for a recent year. State pay data is transmitted to managers operating ONET. 2014 is the first year ONET has included a search window to look up wages by zip code. Data is now available by major cities or regions for many states. This allows smaller firms to drill down to consider market wages for a particular city. A key missing piece in publicly free databases such as ONET is wages by industry. For example, an accountant working in the business office of a manufacturing plant is likely paid less than a similarly educated accountant working in a public accounting firm. Accounting services firms require accountants to work across many industries calling for greater breadth of knowledge. Employers can access market wages by industry via industry trade associations or from large HRM consulting firms.

High versus Low Quality HR Practices

The quality of pay systems depends on structure and design. Lower quality approaches tend to have low levels of definitions for pay levels. A major aim of pay systems is to pay fair wages. Higher quality pay structures define wages by pay grade. Each pay grade has a minimum and maximum pay amount. In these designs, all job titles in a company are assigned to a specific pay grade. Small and medium sized firms often use market wages and assign job titles with similar levels of responsibility to the same grade. For example, all entry level job titles requiring little education or experience are generally assigned to Grade 1 whether the position is in an accounting department, in a housekeeping department, or in a factory within the same organization. See Table 10.1 for a generic pay structure with grades and ranges. The ranges of grades tend be wider for higher grades to accommodate greater variation in duties for higher level job titles. Ranges in higher grades in these designs tend to have an increasing range size from lower to higher grades as shown in the far right column of Table 10.1

Sample Materials: HR Design of Generic Pay Structure with Grades & Ranges

Table 10.1 Generic Pay Grade Structure

Pay Grade	Job Title Cluster	Grade Minimum	Grade Maximum	Range of Grade	Range / Min
Grade 1	Entry Level Positions, Interns	$16,200	$22,200	$6,000 (22,000-16,200)	37%*
Grade 2	Skilled, non-supervisory	$21,100	$29,400	$8,300 (29,400-21,100)	39%
Grade 3	Advanced Skilled, Team Leads	$27,400	$43,700	$16,300 (43,700-27,400)	59%
Grade 4	Supervisors / Junior Managers	$40,500	$66,900	$26,400 (66,900-40,500)	65%
Grade 5	Middle Managers	$58,300	$96,800	$38,500 (96,800-58,300)	66%
Grade 6	Senior Managers	$84,400	$142,000	$57,600 (142,000-84,400)	68%
Grade 7	Executives	$121,000	$210,000	$89,000 (210,000-121,000)	74%

*For example, range width as a percentage: $6,000/$16,200 = 37%

Case: Red Circled Roland

NOTE on Definition of <u>Red-circle status</u>: occurs when an employee's wage is higher than the maximum pay for the grade of his or her job title defined by the pay structure as part of company policy. For example, in Table 10.1, an employee in a job titled "Supervisor" might be paid $67,000 per year. The employee would be deemed red-circled and not eligible for merit increases since his or her maximum pay in Grade 4 was set at $66,900. An employee's pay can move accidentally into red-circle status due to an across the board cost of living pay increase for all or by some error. The red-circle rule is usually enforced for fairness and to keep the system strong to motivate employees, to avoid unfair wages and to meet budget targets (Mathis & Jackson, 2011).

START OF CASE:
Roland was a dedicated, high performing employee and had been with the company for 8 years. He was a Grade 5 in a pay system of 10 grades and was a middle manager supervising six accounting clerks. The clerks processed payroll checks for nearly 1500 employees, and paid vendors for supplies, inventories and service contracts. Roland was in charge of training and managing the clerks along with other accounting duties including preparation of financial reports.

Roland was valued for his knowledge in the payroll system and related software. He reprogrammed the software frequently to comply with changes in the law, such as overtime rules in the Fair labor Standards Act. The clinical organization operated with three shifts seven days a week. Overtime pay occurred every week in many areas. He often worked long hours to do re-programming to accommodate innovative work schedules managers requested to help employees balance work and family life. As a supervisor Roland did not earn overtime pay.

Last year the organization had successfully achieved challenging budget targets. Merit pay raises were more generous for supervisors and managers in recognition of their contributions. However, hospital policy did not allow merit increases to "red-circled" employees. Unfortunately, Roland's pay had somehow moved into a red circled status. He was ineligible for a merit increase. His red circled status caused Melissa, the HR VP, to send an email to her good friend, Diane, the Finance VP to say Roland was not eligible for a merit pay increase. Diane reacted with anger since Melissa knew him well, that he was a top employee and often worked long hours. When Diane confronted Melissa in her office, Melissa said: "I have to do my job. I knew you would stand up for Roland, that's your job as his supervisor. Diane demanded a solution. What could be done?

QUESTIONS to ANSWER
1 Why it is important for organizations to enforce a red-circled policy?

2 Assume the policy is enforced, explain whether you think it is fair or unfair to exclude Roland from the merit pay increase despite his high job performance and commitment.

3 What would you do to solve this case? Can Roland be rewarded somehow without breaking company policy?

1st HR Problem to Solve: Collect Market Wage Data for Retail Job Titles

Collect North Dakota market wages at O*NET for job titles in a retail outlet.

Enter wages in Table 10.2 for the 10th, 50th and 90th percentiles of wages. The low end represents pay for lower education & experience; 90th percentile for high education & experience. Pay grades in the chart may be changed.

INSTRUCTIONS TO COLLECT THE DATA

Go to Occupational Network for wages: http://online.onetcenter.org/ Look for North Dakota 2014

1st Enter a job title in search box at top right corner of main page, a list of related job titles will be shown

2nd Select one job title link that best matches the job title needed.

3rd Scroll nearly to the bottom below the job duty sections; see the "Local Salary" button to find wages by state.

4th Click on drop down arrow to find North Dakota; click "GO" to see state wages.

5th Screen displays annual wage amounts. Enter wages to Table 10.2 below. Data entered for 1st four job titles.

Table 10.2 ONET Market Wage Survey Data for Retail Sector: North Dakota 2014

Job Title	Grade	Low 10th Percentile	Median 50th Percentile	High 90th Percentile	Differences in Market Wages
		Low experience & education, smaller firms	Median experience & education	High experience & education, larger firms	90th percentile minus 10th percentile
Dishwasher	1	$16,000	$18,500	$23,800	$7,800
Cashier	1	$16,400	$20,200	$29,100	$12,700
Floral Designer	1	$16,200	$18,800	$26,300	$10,100
Retail Salesperson	2	$17,100	$23,900	$47,100	$30,000
Stock Clerk	2				
Janitor	2				
Baker	2				
Merchandise Displayer	3				
Shipping Clerk	3				
Butcher	3				
1st Line Supervisor, Retail	4				
1st Line Supervisor, Office	4				
Retail Buyer	4				
HR Specialist	5				
Sales Manager	5				

NOTES: Market wages do not define a logical structure for an individual organization, yet they provide insight. Market wages represent firms of all sizes, strategies, and products and services from low dollar items to items costing thousands of dollars. For example, a small dollar store may look primarily at the 10th percentile wages and to some extent to median wages. The 90th percentile wages likely do not apply.

QUESTIONS to ANSWER

1. What patterns do you see in the data?

2. For each job title subtract the 10th percentile from the 90th percentile and enter the difference in the far right column. What patterns do you see?

Update market wage survey data to estimate wages for a future budget period. This is a necessary step to prepare budgets for upcoming years. The U.S. Bureau of Labor Statistics (www.bls.gov) tracks several indices to apply to the past historical wage amounts at ONET. For example, employers may use recent increases in the Consumer Price Index (CPI) to adjust past wage data. It represents price increases for a market basket of common goods and services. The Bureau of Labor Statistics also tracks increases in wages for geographic regions of the U.S. via the "Employer Cost of Employee Compensation" (ECEC) index. Data for past quarters is available at the website. Due to recent low inflation and wage stagnation in the U.S. associated with the economy, 3.2% is a reasonable estimate to update 2014 ONET wages to budget for a future year (e.g. 2016). To apply this index, the multiplier will be 1.032 times each wage amount. The update has been applied in Table 10.3 below for wages for the first four job titles. The update computation is shown in the row below each updated wage amount.

Fill in Table 10.3 below for the remaining job titles by applying the update factor (3.2%) to the wages collected in Table 10.2

Table 10.3 Updated Wages for Retail Job Titles based on 2014 ONET Market Wages

Job Title	Grade	10th Percentile	Median	90th Percentile
Dishwasher	1	$16,512	$19,092	$24,562
		16,000 x 1.032=	18,500 x 1.032=	23,800 x 1.032=
Cashier	1	$16,925	$20,846	$30,031
		16,400 x 1.032=	20,200 x 1.032=	29,100 x 1.032=
Floral Designer	1	$16,718	$19,402	$27,142
		16,200 x 1.032=	18,800 x 1.032=	26,300 x 1.032=
Retail Salesperson	2	$17,647	$24,665	$48,607
		17,100 x 1.032 =	23,900 x 1.032=	47,100 x 1.032=
Stock Clerk	2			
Janitor	2			
Baker	2			
Merchandise Displayer	3			
Shipping Clerk	3			
Butcher	3			
1st Line Supervisor, Retail Sales	4			
1st Line Supervisor, Office	4			
Retail Buyer	4			
HR Specialist	5			
Sales Manager	5			

BACKGROUND TO BUILD A PAY STRUCTURE

When a firm grows beyond the point where the founder or CEO is no longer able to keep track of each employee's wages and make decisions on pay increases it is time to implement a structured pay system. Structure helps maintain fairness through a system that treats employees consistently. Fair pay levels with a strong pay system can give competitive advantage. In 1914 Henry Ford made a drastic change to the status quo of wage levels. He raised employees pay from $2.25 per day to $5 per day (Worstall, 2012). He was able to attract and retain more talented employees; enjoy higher employee productivity and sustainable competitive advantage compared to other auto makers with lower wage levels. Compensation remains a powerful element of HR practices and organizational strategy today.

Structures of pay grades and pay ranges help organizations achieve the major goals of pay systems: to pay employees fairly and motivate employees; to comply with federal wage laws; and to control budgets. Many organizations have 5 to 10 pay grades. For the large civilian work force employed by the U.S. federal government, the pay system has ten grades, each with 15 steps. At times complex firms have more complex pay structures. Yet, other large firms may keep the structure simple with a few pay grades. Each firm's pay structure tends to be unique from other firms. The guidelines below reflect logical patterns of high quality pay structures in U.S. firms.

TWO GUIDELINES TO BUILD A PAY STRUCTURE

1st Pay range dollar amounts should overlap from grade to grade. For example, Grade 2 minimum pay in Table 10.1 is lower than the maximum for Grade 1. That is, the minimum amount for each grade should be lower than the maximum amount of the preceding lower grade. Overlapping amounts avoid gaps in the pay structure. For example, in Table 10.2 Grade 1 Maximum is $22,600; if Grade 2 minimum were $25,000, employees with wages between $22,601 and $24,999 would be outside any grade, a phantom grade, a design error in the pay structure.

2nd The range (width) of pay grades usually ascends from lower widths to higher widths from low to high grades in a logical pattern. This reflects consistency in the range width to fit differences in market wages based on experience and education and skills requirements. Job titles assigned to lower grades tend to have lower levels of complexity and variation in duties compared to job titles assigned to higher grades. For example, job titles for retail cashier and office clerk in a retail outlet could be in the same pay grade. Each job title requires little education or job experience and market wages for the two job titles are likely in a narrow dollar range. Also, both job titles are entry level with low skills required. At the same time, a marketing manager and a technology manager in the same retail outlet could easily be in a same higher grade compared to entry job titles. The same grade is logical due to similar administrative responsibilities for the two manager positions for decision making, department budgets and supervisory duties. Yet the two job titles represent different fields of expertise in terms of market wages and differences in education, experience and skills required. The range of the pay grade for these two jobs must be wide to accommodate the differences in market wage rates.

HR Design to Create: Prepare a Unique Sample Pay Structure for a Small Retail Outlet

1. Briefly describe firm's products – services: (for example, low cost discount grocery, typical grocery, gourmet grocery

2. Briefly describe firm strategy (e.g. low cost discounted products, average priced consumer goods, high cost unique products)

3. Describe the percentile(s) to focus on to be consistent with firm strategy. NOTE: Market data does not represent a wage structure, yet use insights from ONET data updated in Table 10.3. Follow the two guidelines noted above.

4. List the job titles to assign to each grade below the Table:

Many pay structure designs can be sound and logical for a firm. Some designs will give more competitive edge. It is an error to copy pay rates from Table 10.1 or from the ONET market rates. The pay structure should be consistent with firm strategy.

Grade	Grade Minimum	Grade Maximum	Range of Pay Grade	Grade Width
One				
Two				
Three				
Four				
Five				

Grade One:

Grade Two:

Grade Three:

Grade Four:

Grade Five:

[Intentionally Blank]

[Intentionally Blank]

Chapter 11 Employee Incentives

Introduction with Cause and Effect Relationships

Pay for performance strategies have grown in importance in many industries. These incentive plans are usually based on work output. Incentive pay is also referred to as variable pay, different amounts are paid to each employee for different levels of job performance. Often extra pay in the paycheck gives a person a happy mental boost. It may be a source of fun, pleasure not planned. That is part of the power of incentive pay and the motivational influence it can have. For well-developed plans, Incentive pay is the cause and higher job performance is an outcome in the cause and effect relationship.

Incentives plans work well when tied to organizational goals and strategies and when multiple criteria are the ingredients to assure one goal doesn't work to the detriment of other organizational goals. At times, work output goals focus solely on quantity. However, the quality of output usually falls when quantity is the only incentive requirement. The result can be unfavorable in terms of customer relations for the company. On the other hand, if quality is the single goal, quantity is likely to decline. Multiple strategies covering both quality and quantity are more balanced for overall outcomes to the firm (Marcocchio, 2013).

High versus Low Quality HR Practices

High quality incentive plans for individual employees tend to focus on individual performance, job skills and abilities (Mathis & Jackson, 2011). The requirements to earn a bonus usually require independent actions of each employee. Goals to earn a bonus must be clear. Highly complex plans can fail due to confusion on requirements. Employee competition within a firm can have varying results. Plans tend to work well when all employees in a group have a chance to earn a bonus.

Team goals can also be high quality when employees work interdependently and cooperatively and share information. Team goals tend to be more successful when members have input on the incentive design. An important design issue is how team members share in bonus rewards earned. When team members are paid equally, higher performers in a team may grow frustrated and seek employment where individual bonuses can be earned. Fair pay for individual work is a strong value in the U.S. culture in general. Many organizations pay the rewards of team work on a pro-rata basis with higher performers earning higher portions of a team bonus amount (Mathis & Jackson, 2011).

In general, incentive programs for employees matter. Many firms offer individual bonuses, team bonuses, and organization wide programs such as profit sharing. Incentive plans tend to enhance a firm's ability to attract job applicants, motivate and retain employees. The better incentive plans tie variable pay rewards to specific employee job performance goals. What is measured matters. Incentive goals should be SMART: Specific, Measurable, Achievable, Relevant and Time Oriented with a specific deadline to influence favorable work outcomes.

Sample Materials: HR Design on Simple Individual Bonus Pay

A general concept in bonus plans is that base wages pay for meeting standard work goals; incentives on the other hand, reward performance above and beyond standard work levels.

Table 11.1 Simple Bonus Grid for Individual Employees

	QUALITY REQUIREMENTS (Customer Satisfaction, Lack of Production Errors)			
	Below Standards	Meet Standards	Above Standards	Exceeds Targets (Well Above Standards)
QUANTITY REQUIREMENTS (e.g. Gross sales, Production Output)				
Below Standards	0	0	0	0
Meet Standards	0	0	0	0
Above Standards	0	20% (A)	60%	80%
Exceeds Targets (Well above Standards)	0	40%	80% (B)	100%

Manager A: SAMPLE Bonus Calculation

 Assume the maximum bonus available for Manager A is 7% of wages, with his wages at $60,000.
Assume Manager A performed above standards for quantity but only met requirements for quality requirements as shown by his position in the Bonus Grid in Table 11.1 marked by "(A). What is his bonus?

   Sample Calculation:
   o   What is Manager A's maximum possible bonus?   7% x $60,000 = $4,200

   o   What is Manager A's bonus amount based on his performance scores?   20% x $4,200 = $840

Problem to Solve: Simple Individual Bonus Calculation

   Manager B: Bonus to Solve:

Assume the maximum bonus available for Manager B is 7.5% of wages, with his wages at $70,000.
Assume Manager B exceeded targets for quantity requirements and was above standards for quality requirements.

   o   What is Manager B's maximum possible bonus?

   o   What is Manager B's bonus amount?

72

Table 11.2 Multiple Bonus Criteria: often referred to as a scorecard

Employee Name _Willing Wally__ Supervisor _Pat Fairly_____   Date __July 30__

WORK REQUIREMENTS	Weight	Below Standard 10	Meet Standard 40	Above Standard 80	Exceeds Targets 100	All Points Earned	Points x Weight
Task Quantity	20%		40			40	8
Task Quality	20%			80		80	16
HELPFULNESS							
Help Peers	15%	10				10	1.5
Help Supervisor	15%			80		80	12
OTHER							
Absent	15%			80		80	12
Tardy	5%			80		80	4
Training	10%		40			40	4
Total	100%						57.5%

Assume maximum bonus is $2000. 100% x $2,000 = $2,000

SAMPLE CALCULATION:

What is the bonus amount earned by Willing Wally?   57.5% x $2000 = $1,150

Table 11.3 Problem to Solve: Individual Bonus with Scorecard

Employee Name _Energetic Evan__   Supervisor _Terry Good____   Date Sept 30

Work Requirements	Weight	Below Standard 10	Meet Standard 40	Above Standard 80	Exceed Targets 100	All Points Earned	Points x Weight
Task Quantity	20%			80			
Task Quality	20%				100		
HELPFULNESS							
Help Peers	15%			80			
Help Supervisor	15%			80			
OTHER							
Absent	15%			80			
Tardy	5%			80			
Training	10%		40				
Total	100%						

Assume maximum bonus is $2,000.   100% x $2,000 = $2,000

1 Enter values in Points column on the right.   Calculate points x weight in far right column.

2 What is the bonus amount earned by Energetic Evan?

Sample Materials: Work Group Incentive – Gainsharing Program

Employees share in gains via employees suggestions to improve work processes. A bonus is earned after approved suggestions are implemented and actual costs achieve target levels. Two bonus pools may be set up:

  A. Defective Production Output reduced via employee suggestions.
    All suggestions must be reviewed & approved by an executive group to implement.
  B. Materials Wasted via employee reduced via employee suggestions.
    All suggestion's must be reviewed & approved by an executive group to implement.

Total Savings achieved are determined by the Accounting Department, and divided as follows:
40% to a company reserve account for maintenance, future growth and technology upgrades
60% to employee bonus pool accounts

Group Bonus Earned is shared based on each employee's wages as % of Total Group wages of $3,000,000
Example: Employee "X" earns wages of $45,000: 45,000 / $3,000,000 = 1.5%, the share "X" earns of group bonus.
    Assume amount group earned and deposited to bonus pool is $100,000:
        1.5% x $100,000 = $1,500 is shared with employee "X"

Table 11.4 Sample Gainsharing Program

Defective Production Bonus Pool Results	Amount	Wasted Materials Bonus Pool Results	Amount
Target Defective Production (use prior year actual results)	$900,000	Target Wasted Materials (use prior Year results)	$500,000
Actual Defective Output This year	$700,000	Actual Wasted Materials This year	$440,000

QUESTIONS to ANSWER

		Defective Output	Wasted Materials

1. What are saving by bonus pool? __$200,000____   ___$60,000____
    ($900,000 - $700,000 = $200,000; $500,000-$440,000 = $60,000)

2. What savings go to the reserve account by pool?___$80,000____   ___$24,000 ____
    (.4 x $200,000 = $80,000;   .4 x $60,000 = $24,000)

3. What savings go to each employee bonus pool? _____$120,000____   ___$36,000_____
    (.6 x $200,000 = $120,000; .6 x $60,000 = $36,000)

4. What are group's savings from both pools to share among employees? $120,000 + $36,000 =

                    __$156,000___

    CALCULATE Joe's share of the group bonus from the savings pools. His wages are $60,000.

5. What % is Joe's wages to total work group wages? $60,000/ $3,000,000=   ___2%_____

6. What $ amount is Joe's share of the bonus?   2% x $156,000=   ___$3,120_____

Problem to Solve: Work Group Incentive – Gainsharing Program

Employees share in gains when actual costs are below target levels for two bonus pools:
- Defective Production Output reduced via employee suggestions.
  - All suggestions reviewed & approved by executive group to implement.
- -Materials Wasted via employee reduced via employee suggestions.
  - All suggestions reviewed & approved by an executive group to implement.

Total Savings achieved are determined by Accounting Department, and divided as follows:
- 35% to company reserve account for maintenance, future growth & technology upgrades
- 65% to employee bonus pool account

Group Bonus Earned is shared based on each employee's wages as % of Total Group wages of $4,000,000
  Example: Employee "X" earns wages of $45,000   45,000 / $4,000,000 = 1.12%
  Assume group earned a total bonus of $100,000: 1.12% x $100,000 = $1,120 to employee "X"

Table 11.5 Gainsharing Problem to Solve

Defective Production Pool Results	Amount	Wasted Materials Bonus Pool Results	Amount
Target Defective Output (use prior year actuals)	$650,000	Target Wasted Materials (use prior year)	$350,000
Actual Defective Output	$500,000	Actual Wasted Materials	$200,000

QUESTIONS to ANSWER

	Defective Output	Wasted Materials

1. What are total saving the bonus pool?   __$_____   __$_____

2. What savings to the reserve account by pool?___$_____   __$____ ____

3. What savings go to each bonus pool?   ____$_____   __$_____

4. What are group's savings from both pools to share among employees?

                                 __$_____

CALCULATE Joe's share of the group bonus from the savings pools. His wages are $60,000.

5. What % is Joe's wages to total work group wages?   ___%_____

6. What $ amount is Joe's share of the bonus?   ___$_____

[Intentionally Blank]

References

Aasland, M.S., Skogstad, A., Notelaers, G., Nielsen, M.B., & Einarsen, S. 2010. The prevalence of destructive leadership behavior. *British Journal of Management*, 21, 438–452

Allen, D.G., Mahto, R.V. & Otondo, R.F. 2007. Web-based recruitment: Effects of information, organizational brand, and attitudes toward a web site on applicant attraction. *Journal of Applied Psychology,* 2007, 92(6):1696–1708.

Ashforth, B. 1994. Petty tyranny in organizations. *Human Relations*, 47(7): 755-778.

Bishop, J.W. & Scott, K.D. 2000. An Examination of organizational and team commitment in a self-directed team environment. *Journal of Applied Psychology,* 85(3): 439-450.

Brown, T.C. & Latham, G.P. 2002. The effectiveness of behavioral outcome goals, learning goals and urging people to do their best on an individual's teamwork behavior in a group problem-solving task. *Canadian Journal of Behavioral Science,* 34(4): 276-285.

Brown, T.C. 2003. The effect of verbal self-guidance training on collective efficacy and team performance. *Personnel Psychology*, 56:935 – 964.

Carnol, A. 2015. Inside the STAR interview approach: What you need to know. *Huffington Post,* huffingtonpost.com, Accessed July 2015.

Custance, C. 2014. The real hockeytown USA. *Espn.go.com*. Accessed July 2015.

Downey, S.N., van der Werff, L. & Thomas, K.M. 2015. The role of diversity practices and inclusion in promoting trust and employee engagement. *Journal of Applied Social Psychology,* 45: 35-44.

Eisenberger, R., Stinglhamber, F., Vandenberghe, C., Sucharski, I.L. & Rhoades. L. 2002. Perceived supervisor support: Contributions to perceived organizational support and employee retention. *Journal of Applied Psychology, 87(3): 565–573*

Equal Employment Opportunity Commission (EEOC). *Charge statistics FY 1997 through FY 2014.* http://www.eeoc.gov/eeoc/statistics/enforcement/charges.cfm Accessed July, 2015.

Frayne, C.A. & Geringer, J.M. 2000. Self-management training for improving job performance: A field experiment involving salespeople. *Journal of Applied Psychology*, 85(3): 361-372.

Fried, Y. & Ferris, G.R. 1987. The validity of the job characteristics model: A review and meta-analysis. *Personnel Psychology*, 40(2): 287-322.

Hackman, J.R. & Oldham, G.R. 1980. *Work redesign.* Philippines, Addison-Wesley Publishing

Heneman, H.G., Judge, T.A. & Kammeyer-Mueller, J.D., 2012. *Staffing organizations*. Middleton, WI: McGraw Hill Irwin

Hunter, J.E. 1980. *Validity generalization for 12,000 jobs: An application of synthetic validity generalization to the GeneralAptitude Test Battery (GATB).* Washington, DC: U. S. Department of Labor Employment Service.

Hunter, J.J. & Hunter R.F. 1984. Validity and utility of alternative predictors of job performance. *Psychological Bulletin, 96,* 72-98.

Huselid, M.A. 1995. The impact of human resource management practices on turnover, productivity, and corporate financial performance. *Academy of Management Journal, 3(3):* 635-672

Jelley, R.B., Goffin, R.D., Powell, D.M. & Heneman, R.L. 2012. Incentives and alternative rating approaches: Roads to greater accuracy in job performance assessment? *Journal of Personnel Psychology,* 11(4):159–168

Jelley, R.B. & Goffin, R.D. 2001. Can performance-feedback accuracy be improved? Effects of rater priming and rating-scale format on rating accuracy. *Journal of Applied Psychology,* 86(1): 134-144

Klien, H.J. & Weaver, N.A. 2000. The effectiveness of an organizational level orientation training program in the socialization of new hires. *Personnel Psychology,* 53: 47 – 66.

Martocchio, J.J. 2013. *Strategic compensation.* Upper Saddle River, NJ: Pearson.

Mayo, E. 1947. *The political problem of industrial civilization.* Boston, Division of Research, Graduate School of Business Administration, Harvard University.

Mathis, R.L. & Jackson, J.H. 2011. *Human resource management.* Mason, OH: Southwestern-Cengage Learning.

McDaniel, M.A., Schmidt, F.L. & Hunter, J.E. 1994. A meta-analysis of the validity of methods for rating training and experience in personnel selection. *Personnel Psychology,* 47,283-314.

McKay, P.F., Avery, D.R., & Morris, M.A. 2009. A tale of two climates: Diversity climate from subordinates' and managers 'perspectives and their role in store unit sales performance. *Personnel Psychology,* 62: 767-791.

Miller, L. 2014. State of industry report: Spending on employee training remains a priority. *Association for Talent & Development,* www.td.org/Publications/Magazines/TD/TD   Archive/2014

O*NET, *Occupational Network Online,* onetonline.org. U.S. Department of Labor, National Center for O*NET Development. Accessed July, 2015

Ones, D.S., Viswesvaran, C. & Schmidt, F.L. 1993. Comprehensive meta-analysis of integrity test validities: Findings and implications for personnel selection and theories of job performance. *Journal of Applied Psychology Monograph, 78,* 679-703.

Pew Research Center, 2012. *In changing news landscape even television is vulnerable.* Pewresearch.org. Accessed July, 2015.

Schrader, B.W. & Steiner, D.D. 1996. Common comparison standards: An approach to improving agreement between self and supervisory performance ratings. *Journal of Applied Psychology.* 81(6): 813-820

U.S. Bureau of Labor Statistics. 2015. *Employer Costs for Employee Compensation: March 2015,* online news release issued June 10, 2015. www.bls.gov/news.release/ecec.nr0.htm. Accessed July 2015.

Worstall, T. 2012. The story of Henry Ford's $5 a day wages. *Forbes:* www.forbes.com

Made in the USA
Middletown, DE
24 August 2019